The Substance of Faith
and Other Cotton Patch Sermons
By Clarence Jordan

The Substance of Faith
and Other Cotton Patch Sermons
By Clarence Jordan

Edited by Dallas Lee

A Koinonia Publication

ASSOCIATION PRESS/New York

The Substance of Faith
and Other Cotton Patch Sermons by Clarence Jordan

International Standard Book Number: 0-8096-1843-5
Library of Congress Catalog Card Number: 74-189013

Library of Congress Cataloging in Publication Data

Jordan, Clarence.
  The substance of faith.

  1. Baptists—Sermons. 2. Sermons, American.
I. Title.
BX6333.J76S9   252'.06'132   74-189013
ISBN 0-8096-1843-5

For Florence Jordan,
Who enriched the life of this teacher.

PRINTED IN THE UNITED STATES OF AMERICA

CONTENTS

Introduction 7

I. Incarnational Evangelism

The Womb of God 12
The Sons of God 17
The Humanity of God 24
Incarnational Evangelism 31

II. The Substance of Faith

The Substance of Faith 39
The Adventures of Three Students
  in a Fiery Furnace 46

III. The God Movement

The Demonstration Plot 56
The Lesson on the Mount—I 62
The Lesson on the Mount—II 69
Was Jesus Really Poor? 78
The Currency of the Kingdom 88

IV. The Distinct Identity

Metamorphosis 94
Jesus Christ Revealed 97
The Mind of Christ in the Racial Conflict 104
Making a Habit of Love 112

V. Persisting Threats to Authentic Faith

An Ancient Heresy Incarnate 120
Judas 124
Taking the Name in Vain 134

VI. God's Destination for Man

The Meaning of the Sabbath 144
The Father's Pursuing Love 148
The Death of Jesus 152
Persisting in Love 155
A Spirit of Partnership 159

INTRODUCTION

Years ago, before Southern churches exhibited such a fear of him, Clarence Jordan went before a Southern congregation and spoke of the spirit of brotherhood alive in the New Testament.

After the sermon an elderly woman, as crisp with pride as a dead honeysuckle vine, made her way down the aisle, her blazing eyes telegraphing the tone of her response. Clarence braced, and she delivered—straight from the gut level of her culture:

"I want you to know that my grandfather fought in the Civil War, and I'll never believe a word you say."

Clarence, who was tall and gracious and as Southern as sow belly himself, smiled and replied:

"Ma'am, your choice seems quite clear. It is whether you will follow your granddaddy or Jesus Christ."

Clarence knew, from the pure-deep streams of his own heritage, that the ghosts of old Confederate grandfathers still manipulated the spirits of a people, somehow making it possible for them to voice obedience to this radical Jesus on the one hand, and yet cling to a deadening web of tradition on the other.

It was spiritual schizophrenia. But the churches, professing to be the body of Christ, seemed to offer no counsel toward restoration of mental health. A culture had appropriated a religion and the name of its Lord without resistance, and continued daily to establish firmer precedent, justifying its violent existence with the self-proclaimed approval of God.

Clarence grew up in south Georgia and somehow managed to gain the clear vision to perceive this unholy alliance. At the University of Georgia's School of Agriculture and at Southern Baptist Theological Seminary's graduate program in Greek New Testament, he equipped himself to speak to the situation. In 1942 he established Koinonia Farm in south Georgia as an experiment in Christian communal living. The intention was to give flesh as well as voice to the basic ideas of peace and love and sharing—ideas which call men to acknowledge that in Christ the walls of culture, race, and status are down.

Clarence, his wife Florence, and others who joined them sought to be a part of the economic and religious life of the South, and yet remain distinct as committed followers of Jesus. They obviously succeeded in focusing their lives on the sensitive spot in the culture. When the experiment in community began giving visibility to their beliefs (Black people *were* welcomed into the fellowship, possessions *were* relinquished, and men *did* go to prison rather than co-operate with the military), they fell victim to the "race-mixing Communist" epithet and violent hostility. The scandalous affair between the church and the culture had been exposed and threatened. The battle was on.

As the Koinonia community endured physical violence and economic boycott, Clarence's communication grew bolder and more prophetic. He began translating his own Cotton Patch versions of the New Testament books with the hope that he could make people feel like participants in the New Testament drama, rather than like spectators. Translating the ideas more than the words of the New Testament, he set the gospel story in twentieth-century Georgia and sought to recount New Testament episodes in ways that would leapfrog the centuries and confront modern-day America with the mind of this man Jesus. All Scripture references in this book are either just as Clarence Jordan read them, freely translating from a Greek New Testament as he spoke; or they are taken from *The Cotton Patch Versions of Paul's Epistles, Luke-Acts, Matthew and John,* published by Association Press, New York; or they are from pamphlets such as *Letters From Partners,* the Cotton Patch version of I, II Peter; I, II, III John; and Jude, printed by Koinonia Partners.

To him, a failure to read the Bible with a sense of participation and imagination helped to explain the great distance that separated the ideas of the New Testament from the activities of twentieth-century churches. And such cold reading also helped explain what he considered to be the fundamental error of modern American churchism: the constant emphasis on the deity of Jesus to the point of obscuring the humanity of God. Most churchmen, he felt, spent so much energy trying to assure themselves of the deity of Jesus that they in fact denied the humanity of God in the process. And the humanity of God, Clarence believed, was what the incarnation was all about.

All across the country, from 1942 until his death at Koinonia Farm in the fall of 1969, Clarence proclaimed an incarnational faith—a faith that took shape in the life-styles, actions, and attitudes of people. The Scriptures were alive in the man and in his experiences, and the power of his proclamations restored a sense of excitement to thousands whose faith had grown stale.

He seldom spoke from the confines of a written manuscript.

Working from a brief outline scribbled on the back of an envelope or on an old purchase order from the farm, or on a sheet of hotel stationery, he would just start rolling, speaking his mind in the context of the moment, staying close to some New Testament text, hoping that the ideas would take root in his listeners and be cultivated in personal ways.

When he spoke, he communicated all over. The message was in his tone, in his motions, in his eyes, in his often deliberate stumbling misuse of words, and most of all in his spirit. His brand of communication was meant to be heard and felt and tasted—in short, experienced. When you heard him you didn't just get new information or a new scholarly angle on some theological issue. You encountered a man—a man who strove to live by what he was talking about; a tall, country man with a big Southern voice, an infectious sense of humor, and a penetrating social compassion that balanced his evangelical warmth with ethical dynamite.

So, in a real sense, this book of edited communication from Clarence Jordan is an intrusion on the unique relationships he developed with his audiences. It was a deeply felt responsibility to select and edit for reading this small portion from the volumes of material captured over the years by tape recorder. I did not attempt to condense into one book everything the man said. Rather, I sought to select lectures and portions of talks and discussions that seemed to communicate the essence of the man's faith, what he perceived to be the purpose and activity of God in the world, and how he viewed the responsibility of those who claimed to be followers of Jesus. Mostly, I worked with transcripts of lectures made during the last decade of his life before church conferences, ministerial study groups, and congregations.

The brief statement that closes this book is the vision that burned in Clarence most of his life. Koinonia Partners grew out of that vision and seeks today to give it expression through a Fund for Humanity which is supported by thousands of "partners" across the land as well as by the shared profits of farming and industries at Koinonia.

Through the fund, houses are built and sold to the rural disinherited at cost with no-interest loans; industries are established to provide jobs for the low-skilled; land is provided for farming "by virtue of usership rather than ownership"; and a communication ministry is sustained that is grounded in the idea that incarnational faith—faith rooted in action—is the way for man to rediscover a sense of partnership with God and with his fellow men.

The rich and the poor, the educated and uneducated, the skilled and the unskilled are coming together in a spirit of partnership under God.

Clarence Jordan was a man of shifting moods and passions. He grieved deeply over the stubborn will of many people in his homeland. And yet his life seemed to be a process of grief being consumed by celebration. With all the sorrow that came from the rejection and hostility he experienced, there also came unique joys and a strong aura of manhood that even his enemies spoke of reverently. He seemed to be a personal exhibit that fullness of life did lie in the way of following this man Jesus uncompromisingly.

There was scholarship in his head, the excitement of confrontation in his posture, the integrity of practicing what he preached in his countenance; there was humbleness and gentle love in his spirit. And there was reservoired deep in his soul, like a great valley of water behind a tiny dam, a celebration of life. For all the anger he expressed, for all the grief he shared, for all the thunder he delivered, there was the feeling that he sought to share *good news*— not to keep a wrathful God from condemning someone to eternal fires, but to say, "Here are ideas for life—not death; ideas a loving God has given to us all. We have tried them and found them fulfilling. For God's sake and yours, give them a chance to find expression in your life."

Woven inextricably into the words of this book, then, is the life of a great man of faith. My advice is: look closely, listen carefully, make ready to think, and to laugh, cry or get angry, for this man will speak to you now.

Dallas Lee

I

Incarnational Evangelism

*"I don't think we have a right
to bear witness to that which we do not
experience. The incarnation is
the announcement of the
Good News as fact."*

THE WOMB OF GOD

Today when the Church is being attacked and challenged on every hand as a viable institution, when the Church is in doubt and confused about its own identity and mission, it must make contact—it must touch base—with the rock from which it was hewn. We must look again into the faces of that crowd of witnesses which surrounds us and cheers us on in our often lonely task of being faithful witnesses to the Lord Jesus.

When the Church is facing such tremendous problems, it cannot afford to go off half-cocked. Today we are facing the problems of militarism and violence. We are facing the problem of poverty. And we are facing an even more grievous sickness in our culture—that of wealth. All of these things are greatly affecting us today, and we are getting anxious to get up and get on and do something, do something, do something quick! I do not want the Church to go off half-cocked, for I know how frustrating it can be for it to get out to do the work of God without the presence of God and without the power of God. Jesus said something about seeds falling on rocky ground where they sprouted quickly. They came up, they passed resolutions, they organized committees, they went out and visited, and they set up study commissions, and they made little tours to see what the problems were. But when it came to getting down to *dealing* with those problems, then they withered and dried up because, Jesus said, they had no depth of root. Sometimes I hear ministers haranguing their congregations, "Do something! Do something!" It's about like trying to automate a bunch of corpses. We just aren't ready to do anything. We're dead. We've got to have the power of the spirit from on high that will make us live beings, and then, I think, we can get on with the Father's business.

So I'm going back to the Book of Acts to help you drink from the spring, the refreshing waters that will give you strength for the hours of heat and scorching sun, that we may be faithful witnesses in these hours that are troubling our souls and challenging our very existence.

I want to start reading from the Book of Acts. My method for this will be exegetical, rather than homiletical, although I doubt that I'll be able to resist the impulse to cut loose every now and then with a little south Georgia preaching. Now, if my words sound a little bit queer and funny to your ear, a little bit jumbled and slangy, it will be because I am either reading directly from the Greek text and translating it off the cuff, or reading from the manuscript of the *Cotton Patch Version of Luke and Acts.* This *Cotton Patch Version* is an effort to translate the Scriptures for humble cotton-picking Christians who haven't been able to understand what their pea-picking preachers have been saying.

Reading from the first chapter in the Book of Acts: *I wrote the first volume, Friend of God, about the many deeds and lessons which Jesus got under way, up to the day when he ascended. Prior to this he had given, through the Holy Spirit, specific orders to his special agents, and had shown himself to them with many positive proofs that he was still alive, even after he had been killed. Through forty days he appeared to them and discussed matters concerning the God Movement. And while staying with them, he urged them not to leave Atlanta, but to wait for the Father's promised gift about which he had told them. "Yes, John dipped people in water,"* he said, *"but in just a few days you all will be dipped in Holy Spirit."*

Luke is saying that he has written a previous volume. He wrote the first volume, he said, to tell about all those things which Jesus got in motion, as if to infer that the second volume is to tell you about those things which Jesus *still* is getting in motion. The first volume is a biography of the life of Jesus in human flesh in one body. The second volume is the life of Jesus in his resurrected body, in his new body, after he had convinced them that he was still very much alive, in the body which Paul called the Church. So the first volume is a biography of Jesus of Nazareth. The second volume is the biography of Jesus working through the Church.

You will note a very close similarity between these two biographies. Both give birth narratives. In the first volume, Mary is his mother. In the second volume, the Church takes the place of Mary and God implants his Holy Spirit in the Church to bring forth a new kind of Son of God on the face of the earth, and it's that Son of God who is still up to his old work—preaching, teaching, and healing. So the Book of Acts is going to tell us about Jesus who has been raised from the dead, who's alive and still up to his old works, working now not through one body—Jesus of Nazareth— but through many bodies which make a whole—his Church.

The first volume comes to a fitting climax in the Ascension. Luke tells about the birth of this young fellow, how he lived and moved among us, what the reaction of the world was to him, how finally the world killed him, but how God raised him from the dead and then the curtain falls with him going into the realm of the spirit—not up to heaven as we are led to believe, but moving into the realm of the spirit; not leaving us here on earth, but being with us in a more real way than while he was limited to just one body.

Through forty days after his resurrection, he appeared to them and discussed matters concerning the God Movement.

This forty days would mean something to his disciples. The period of time with forty days was significant to Jewish people. It was for forty days that it rained upon the earth. This period of forty days always meant a wilderness experience—a time of being subdued, but a time of great expectation for something mighty to happen. After the forty days of rain upon the earth, the ark settled and Noah got out and the world began to be populated again. Here was a great burst of activity after a time of being subdued. Then out of the forty years in the wilderness came a time of great expansion and blossoming and the children of God moved into the Promised Land, and God walked with them and they became his people. Then there were forty days when our Lord went into the wilderness and was tempted by the evil one. His soul was tried to its very depths. But then, after that wilderness experience, there comes a great burst of spiritual activity, and something mighty begins to happen. He begins preaching: "Change your way of living, restructure your life, for the new order of the Spirit is at hand!"

And now, we have another forty days—a grave experience. Crucified, subdued, but waiting for something mighty to happen— and it *will* happen in just a little while.

And while staying with them he urged them not to leave, but to wait for the Father's promised gift, about which he had told them.

Wait a minute now, don't get too anxious to solve all the world's problems. Waiting until you're clothed with power from on high can be a very important part of solving these problems.

So those about him began asking, "Will that be the occasion on which you will take over the government? Are you going to come with great clouds and power and set yourself up and rule for a thousand years? Is this what you're talking about?" And Jesus said to them, "You are not to get all worked up about time tables and events which the Father has under his own control. But as the Holy Spirit comes over you, you will get power and will be my martyrs, my living examples, in Jerusalem and Samaria, and to the uttermost parts of the land." As he went away, and while they were still staring into the sky, two men in blue jeans joined them and said, "You Georgia people, why are you standing there looking at the sky?"

You know, it's so much more pleasant to be sky people than it is to be earth people. It's so much more pleasant to worship Jesus going away than it is to incarnate him coming after us. We want the Lord to be in his Holy Temple and let all the earth keep silent before him. We want to stare into the sky. But men with blue jeans come and say, "Come on, men. Get your eyes out of the sky. Get your working britches on. We got work to do!"

Then they returned to Atlanta from Peach Orchard Hill which is in the suburbs of Atlanta. When they got back, they went upstairs where they were living. This included Rock and Jack and Jim and Andy, Phil and Tom, Bart and Matt, Jim Alston and Simon the Rebel and Joe Jameson. All of them, including the women and Mary, Jesus' mother, and his brothers, were continually praying together.

Now this is a most significant part of this whole bit. We've got the eleven there. They've been with him through all his ministry. They know what he did in Volume One. They are knowing that their task is to be Volume Two. They are to carry on the ministry of their Lord. But now they've got somebody else with them. They've got Mary, Jesus' mother, and his brothers. Now we've got Mary beginning to really become Jesus' mother. She was told in Volume One that she would give birth to a son and that son would be the Son of the Most High and that a sword would pierce her heart. She learned later that the sword that pierced her heart was the babe that was formed in her womb. And she tried to keep him. She was told that he was God's son, but the mother instinct in her wanted to keep him. She wanted him for *her* son. When she went to the temple with him when he was twelve years old, and he got interested in the ministerial association meeting and didn't get with them on the way back, she then came in a great fluster of anger and said to him, "What's the matter with you?! Your daddy and I have been looking for you all over everywhere and here you are at the ministerial meeting. Why did you grieve us like that?!" Now, she was saying to him, "You're my son." He was saying to her, "Yes, Mother, I am your son. But I am my Father's son also. Didn't you know that I had to be about my Father's business?" And Luke says she didn't understand about that.

Later on, after he had been preaching and getting himself into trouble, perhaps having been investigated by the House Un-Roman Activities Committee, and right in the shadow of the cross, his mother and his brothers come to him and I know what they want with him. They want to say, "Now look, Jesus. You are about to take this thing too far. You come on home and be a good boy. We can give you a job as foreman in the woodworking division of the carpenter shop. And I want you to forget about all of this business of being the messiah, and all like that." I know what this mother and these brothers wanted. They wanted to keep him in the family! But Jesus' word to them was, "Who is my mother, and my brother, and my sister? He that does the will of my Father. He is my mother, and my brother and my sister."

Now, when we get over finally to the crucifixion, when Mary relinquished him and gave him away, gave him to mankind as God intended him to be, at last when she lost him, she became his mother.

The Church, in a very real sense, gives birth to sons of God. She is the womb in which they are conceived. In my own case this was true. The little Baptist church in which I grew up nurtured me. In its womb I learned the Scriptures. I suckled at its breasts. And the little church thought that it not only was my mother, but also my father. And when I began to go about my Father's business, the Church said, "No, son, you're piercing our hearts. We don't want to give you up." And when I finally persisted in going about my Father's business, my mother, the Church, renounced me.

It's hard for a mother whose womb conceives a child of God to quit being a mother and let that son get about his Father's business. I think this is the real tension between preachers and their congregations today. Preachers are nourished in the Church. They're educated by it. They love it. It has been the umbilical cord to life for them. And yet when they get on about their Father's business, maybe getting in jail, getting in demonstrations, spending themselves to do the will of the Father, the Church says, "No, son; come be my son. Stop being so much like your Father." The preacher has to say, "No, mother. I must be about my Father's business."

I think this is the trouble of our youth today. We have been too successful with our religious education. We have finally gotten our children to catch the point! And so they get the idea that God is to be obeyed. He is to be followed. And when these kids get out with visions in their heads and dreams in their hearts and start following the very God we have fathered and nurtured within them, then we say, "No, son; be my son. Don't be so much like your Father."

At long last, though, Mary learned to be the mother of Jesus by giving him to mankind to do his Father's business. And I hope and pray that before I pass on to glory, the little church that expelled me from its fellowship will realize that I really am its son, that I really do love it and that it will gather with me, perhaps even after the crucifixion, along with the rest of the brethren and realize that you can only be the true mother of a child of God when you relinquish your motherhood and give him to all mankind. For God did not give his son to the Church. He did not give his son to Mary. She was the mere instrument through which he came. God gave his son to the world. And when our sons and daughters give themselves with an abandon to following their Father in the lowly paths of the world, let not the Church hold back and say, "Come, children; be your mother's children." Let us grasp their hands, seeing in them the image of their Father, and say to them, "Son, though it leads you to a cross, be a good son of your daddy."

THE SONS OF GOD

We saw that Luke had written a two-volume biography of the life of Jesus. The first volume deals with the life of Jesus in the one man—Jesus of Nazareth. And the second volume deals with the life of Jesus in his new body—the Church.

In the first volume, Mary is the instrument through which the Spirit of God invades the earth and becomes flesh. In the second document, Mary is replaced by the Church. In the first account, Mary tries to possess her son. In the second account, she realizes that she can possess him only by surrendering him as God's gift to mankind. And so we closed with Mary, Jesus' mother, gathered with the twelve, waiting expectantly.

Now, there is to be in the second account a virgin birth also, a divine impregnation in which the virgin shall conceive and bring forth a son. And we cannot understand this unless we go back a bit and look at the Gospel of Luke and see how the first account occurred. Now, you might be a little uneasy by the fact that I'm even mentioning the virgin birth. Most liberals today have been either too lazy or too stupid to examine this doctrine to find out what it's all about. They have been embarrassed by the fact that they cannot understand it from a scientific standpoint. And the conservatives have zealously affirmed it; although, as usual, they have fervently affirmed something they did not understand. So both the liberals and conservatives are hung up on what was to the Church one of its most precious ideas—that of the virgin birth. I want us to look at it and see if we cannot restore it to its proper and rightful place in our thinking.

Reading from the first chapter of Luke, the 26th verse:

Now in the sixth month—that is, the sixth month of pregnancy of Elizabeth—*a messenger, Gabriel, was sent from God to a city in Galilee.* (Notice the direction of the action. It is from heaven, earthward. Not vice versa.) *He was sent to a city by the name of Nazareth to a young lady who was engaged to a man by the name of Joseph, who was of the House of David, and the name of the young lady was Mary. And he entered to her and said, "Hello, you most favored one. The Lord is with you." And she was just bowled over at that greeting and she began to wonder what in the world this salutation meant. And the messenger said to her, "Stop trembling, Mary, for you have found favor with God. For behold you shall become pregnant and give birth to a boy. And you shall call his name, Jesus. He shall be great and shall be called the Son of the Most High. And the Lord God will give to him the throne of his father David, and he shall rule over the house of Jacob into the ages. And of his kingdom there shall be no end." And Mary said to the angel, "How shall this be, since I have not known man?" And the messenger said to her, "Holy Spirit shall come upon you and power of the Most High shall overshadow you. Wherefore that Holy Thing which is sired in you shall be called God's boy. Now behold Elizabeth, your kinsman, has conceived in her old age and this is now the sixth month for her who was called barren." Then Mary said, "Behold the handmaiden of the Lord. Let it be unto me according to your word."*

Here we have God taking the initiative, coming to earth, impregnating a woman and siring a son. That's the narrative. Now we say, how can it be? And we get scientific about it. How can that happen? I don't know. We're not involved here with scientific fact. We're involved with something much more important than that. We're involved with religious truth. When you are dealing with religious truth, you're plumbing the depths of man's soul and you cannot be bound by mere little old scientific fact.

That's too little. You've got to break out and go beyond that. Now religious truth, while going beyond scientific fact, still must be truth. We all know that the account of Daniel in the lions' den —the three young men in the fiery furnace—is not scientific fact. But it is religious truth. It reveals the truth about God and about man to such a vast extent that if you were confined to just mere scientific fact, you couldn't plumb the depths of either God or man. We know the parable of the Good Samaritan is not historical fact. There perhaps was no man going from Jerusalem to Jericho. But the parable of the Good Samaritan is true, much more so than if we could establish that it was historical fact. We know the parable of Lazarus and Dives is not historical fact. Jesus never intended it to be such. But it is religious truth far beyond any truth it might have contained if it had been scientific fact.

So, I'm not worried about whether this is scientific fact or not. I'm inclined to believe that Joseph was in the flesh the father of Jesus. I don't think Jesus ever doubted that. But God was his Father in a very real sense. And what the virgin birth is trying to say to us is not that a man became divine, but that God Almighty took the initiative and established permanent residence on this earth!

Now we, today, have reversed the virgin birth. We have reversed the incarnation. Instead of the Word becoming flesh and dwelling among us, we turn it around and we take a bit of flesh and deify it. We have deified Jesus and, thus, effectively rid ourselves of him even more than if we had crucified him. When God becomes a man, we don't know what to do with him. If he will just stay God, like a God ought to be, then we can deal with him. We can sing songs to him if he'll just stay God. If he will stay in heaven and quit coming down to earth and dwelling among us where we have to deal with a baby in a manger and a man on the cross; if God Almighty would just stay God and quit becoming man—then we could handle him. We can build our cathedrals to him. This is the bind we get in today. We reverse the action—from heaven to earth—and we turn it around and build it from earth to heaven. And salvation becomes something that we will attain someday, rather than God coming to earth to be among us. So we build churches, we set up great monuments to God and we reject him as a human being.

A church in Georgia just set up a big $25,000 granite fountain on its lawn, circulating water to the tune of 1,000 gallons a minute. Now that ought to be enough to satisfy any Baptist. But what on earth is a church doing taking God Almighty's money in a time of great need like this and setting up a little old fountain on its lawn to bubble water around? *I was thirsty . . . and ye built me a fountain.* We can handle God as long as he stays God. We can build him a fountain. But when he becomes a man we have to give him a cup of water. So the virgin birth is simply the great transcendent truth that God Almighty has come into the affairs of man and dwells among us.

In the Book of Acts we see this same drama re-enacted. They all are quietly together, the handmaiden of the Lord is praying, saying, "Be it unto me according to your will. I'm ready to be impregnated. I want to be the womb of God. I want to be the agency through which he comes into this world and does his work in the affairs of men. We're ready, Lord, to be impregnated." But something is necessary before this.

While all of this was going on, Rock arose and said to the brotherhood, "Brothers, it was inevitable that David's inspired prediction about Judas being in cahoots with those who framed Jesus should come true. He belonged to our group and thereby obtained a rightful share in this undertaking." It was he, you know, who with his bribe money bought a plot, where he fell and busted open, and his guts spilled out. That's why the people around Atlanta still refer to it as the "Blood Plot."

Now this is an interesting statement. It says Judas fell and busted open and his guts spilled out. Here I think we have a clue as to why Judas really betrayed his Lord. He's a man who has been subjected to great tension—the pull of Jesus Christ (the prophetic message of the Gospel) and the pull of Caiaphas the high priest. The pull of this professional religious establishment and the pull of this prophetic Gospel pulled the man in two and broke him. His body symbolized what had already happened to his spirit. Judas was what we might call a busted gut Christian. And let me tell you his number is legion.

Rock continued, "In the book of Psalms it says, 'May his barn be empty and his house be vacant,' and, 'Let someone else take over his office.' So, we've got to choose someone to join with us as evidence of Jesus' aliveness. Someone who has been with us throughout the whole time Jesus was among us—from the beginning at John's baptism until the day of his ascension."

Now if his body is to be impregnated it's got to be a normal body. Part of it has been broken off. And Rock is saying, "We've got to put our body together." This body that Jesus is going to come into must be a whole body. Jesus had a passion for wholeness. All of his healing miracles were to make men whole. He never did a miracle and made a man weird. He always made him whole. Take the man with the withered hand—Jesus didn't get in the hand-making business and plaster him with hands. He just made him whole, what he should have been all along. When he opened the eyes of the blind, he didn't get in the eye-making business and plaster them all over the guy. He just made the eyes whole as they should have been all along. And so the body of Christ must be a whole body, no part missing, and Rock is saying, "Look, one part is busted loose. We've got to take another to replace it." And then he said, "Not only that, we've got to find a part that's been with this body ever since the baptism of John unto the ascension." The whole drama has got to be re-enacted with a new body.

So they nominated two—George Jones, who was nicknamed Barsey, and Matt. They prayed and said, "You, Lord, heart-knower of all, please make clear which one of these two you have selected to receive the rightful share of this undertaking and commission from which Judas deserted to go his own way." They had them draw lots, and the share fell to Matt, who then was counted in with the eleven officers.

Now you've got the whole body. It's ready to be impregnated. It is saying, "I am your handmaiden. Impregnate me. Let me be the mother of God." And this is exactly what begins to happen. This is the job of the Church. To become the womb of God through which he can bring his child into this world.

Now, the early Church was willing to become pregnant. But I think the trouble with God's bride today is that she either has passed the menopause or she's on the pill. Or perhaps even worse, she's gone a-whoring. It could be that she has sought other husbands, that she's trying to let someone else impregnate her. And generally when a woman goes a-whoring and becomes pregnant, she hopes that the offspring will favor her, rather than the father. And I think this is what's happening many times in the Church today. It isn't that we are failing to beget children. We are begetting children. But they are not bearing the image of the Almighty. They are bearing the image of false gods. I think one of those false gods that the Church is whoring with is a god by the name of Mammon. And a lot of his children are bearing his image in high places. I read where a great denomination met and the president of that denomination stayed in the swankiest suite in the swankiest hotel. I'm not too sure that that child is in the image of the Almighty God whose boy was so poor he had nowhere to lay his head. We'd better be careful, friends. We're begetting children, but I wonder if they aren't bearing the image of their true father—Mammon—and not Jehovah.

Now, the Church is ready for the Spirit to come upon it, and so: *When the day of Pentecost arrived, they were all gathered in one place. Then all of a sudden there came from the sky a rumbling of a mighty rushing wind and it filled the whole house where they were gathered. And they saw forked flames as from a fire, and it stayed with each of them. Everybody was bursting with Holy Spirit and started talking in whatever different languages the Spirit directed.*

Now you get the picture? It's on the day of Pentecost. Why the day of Pentecost? What is Pentecost? That's the fiftieth day. That's the day that symbolizes the Year of Jubilee. You know, the

Hebrews had every seventh day as the sabbath day; then every seventh week was the sabbath week, every seventh year was the sabbath year, and then, when you had a cycle of seven sevens, that made 49. The 49th year was the usual sabbath, but then they took the 50th year to make a special year. And that was the Year of Jubilee. On that year, the land returned to its original holders. The captives were set free. Debts were forgiven. The prisons were open. It was a new deal, a new era coming in. And the Day of Pentecost was a symbol of the Year of Jubilee, of the new deal, of the new order, when God would set things aright.

This was the day when the Church was born. It was symbolized by the coming of two things—wind and fire. The wind came as a mighty, rushing wind. Now the Spirit of God is not a little gentle spring zephyr blowing over the face of somnolent saints. The Spirit of God is a mighty, rushing wind—wind in a hurry. And wind in a hurry is a hurricane, smashing through the whole house, not filling just the pulpit, but also the pews. Filling the whole house. There's something about wind that goes into every nook and cranny. The Spirit of God, when it impregnates the Church, leaves not one little bit of it unturned. It cannot impregnate the pulpit without also impregnating the pews. It's a mighty, rushing wind. And then, Luke says, it was like forked tongues of fire. (Wind and fire. Now, ever since Pentecost a lot of us have been pretty long on the wind, and a little bit short on the fire.)

But what is that fire? He said it was a sustained fire. That it sat upon each one of them. It stayed there. What kind of fire stays upon us? My mama gave me a Bible when I joined the Church at twelve years old, and it had a picture of Pentecost and had all those folks sitting around with great beards and hair and each one of them had his own little private ball of fire sitting on top of his head, licking out tongues. I never could understand why it didn't set all that hair on fire. But that isn't what Luke is talking about here. He's saying that it was a sustained fire. I think he's talking about electrical fire. Jesus Christ had come in the midst of those people. And they had gathered around him. He was like an electrode with an enormous amount of current in it. And when you get another electrode around, one that has great juice in it, the fire will jump from one electrode to the other and it will sit there. Now, I think that's the picture of Pentecost. The Spirit of Jesus with that great energizing power of the Spirit is in the midst of his people. They have gathered around him and the power that was in him, jumped from him to them, and they were energized by the same power, the same fire, that energized him.

So, when these people got the fire into them, they start acting.

They start preaching. They start doing what Jesus had been doing all along. And so they start talking. People gather together and they hear them. And they say: *Look, aren't all these preachers Americans? Then how is it that each of us is hearing it in his own native tongue. French, German, Portuguese, Chinese, Russian, Italian, Greek, Turkish, Burmese, Hebrew, Swedish, Afrikaans—in our own languages we are hearing them tell of God's mighty doings. Everybody was dumfounded and puzzled, saying one to another, "What's the meaning of this?"*

When the Church of God gets to talking it doesn't talk in unknown tongues. It talks in the tongues of people. It talks in their native dialect. It knows how to talk "hippie." It knows how to talk "ministerial." It knows how to talk "laymen." It knows how to talk bum language. It knows how to talk presidential language. It knows how to talk all kinds of language. The spirit of God becomes articulate and speaks the language of people. It doesn't get up in the church with a holy whine and talk about "thee" and "thou" and "what" and "what-not." When the Church becomes articulate, it becomes articulate in the language in which people are born—not some foreign, ministerial kind of language.

I think one of the big troubles with Jesus' sermons was that people could understand them. So the Church is talking not in an unknown tongue now, it's talking in *every* tongue, so that every man can hear the majesties of God.

Everybody was dumfounded and puzzled, saying one to another, "What's the meaning of this?" (We never heard it like that before! We thought the only thing the church could say was its memory verse.) *And others said, "Aw, they're tanked up on white lightnin'." So Rock, along with the eleven, got right up and started explaining matters to them. He said, "Fellow Georgians and all you delegates in Atlanta, let me set you straight on this right now. These folks are not tanked up like you think, because it's just nine o'clock in the morning."* (Rock didn't say these folks don't drink; he just said it's too early.) *"This is the happening described in the book of Joel."*

And then he quotes from Scripture and he says, *" 'When the time is ripe,' says God, 'I will share my spirit with all mankind. And your sons and your daughters will speak the truth. Your young people will catch visions. And your old people will dream dreams.' "*

When you've got young people seeing visions and old people dreaming dreams, you've closed the generation gap! He said, these young people, your daughters, these sons whom I have sired in your womb will begin speaking the truth! They'll put aside all this hypocrisy, all this deceit, all of this tommyrot that we have foisted upon mankind, and they will speak the truth. And then he says: *"Yes indeed, when the time is right, I'll share my spirit with my boys and my girls and they will speak the truth. I will put terrors in the sky above and nightmares on the earth below. Blood and fire and a mushroom cloud. The sun will be turned into blackness, and the moon into blood, when the glory and the majesty of the Lord's era will be ushered in. And then the man who shares in the Lord's nature will come through."*

Then Rock established that Jesus really had risen from the dead, that he was alive and energizing them, and the people cried out, *"Will you please tell us, brothers, what can we do about it?"* And Rock said to them: *"Reorder your lives, and let each of you be initiated into the family of Jesus Christ, so your sins can be dealt with. And you will receive the free gift of the Holy Spirit."*

First you need to be something. You need to be in the family of God. You need to be empowered by the Holy Spirit. Then let the Spirit bear these works.

It's when the Word of God becomes powerful among us, when his spirit becomes energizing in us, creating us into the image of his Son, it is then that the world is faced with the presence of the Lord God Almighty on this earth. He is not in his heaven with all well on the earth. He is on this earth, and all hell's broke loose.

THE HUMANITY OF GOD

We have seen that the parable of the virgin birth symbolizes that when God decided to establish residence upon the earth, he did not come as a foreign missionary for a brief time to bring the light to us and then return on a celestial furlough, nor as an alien asking for acceptance and approval and conforming himself to the customs of his adopted country. But he decided to come as a native-born son, a member of the human family. And that, to me, is what the virgin birth is saying: that God has decided to become a member of the human race, that he's joined with us, that he's blended his genes with our genes to produce a new kind of creature on this earth—a divine-human creature who will have his Father in heaven and his mother on earth and who will set forth to do the will of God.

So, then, the virgin birth is not proof of the deity of Jesus, but, rather, evidence of the humanity of God. It definitely establishes that from here on out we can't deal with God without confronting him in our brother. John bears this out when he says, "And the Idea, the Word, became a human being, and dwelt among us."

The word in the Greek for "dwell among us" is the word *eskēnōsen* which originally meant "to pitch one's tent." In those days these people were wandering nomads and they didn't just take their vacation in tents, they lived in tents. And so they say, "God became one of us and lived among us, pitched his tent in our midst." Now today we might translate it, "And the Word became flesh and parked his mobile home next to ours." Or maybe we would say, "The Word became flesh and bought a home in our neighborhood—yeah, the black bastard, and made the price of our property go down!"

The parable of the great judgment is affirming the truth of the virgin birth—that Jesus Christ is now our brother. He has been born here on the earth into the human family. In the great judgment we have it told that Jesus said, *"I was sick and you visited me, I was naked, I was hungry, I was thirsty, and I was in prison . . ."* and we said, *"Lord, when did we see you naked and sick and hungry and thirsty and in prison?"* And Jesus said, *"Inasmuch as you did it unto one of the least of these my brothers, you have done it unto me."* He was affirming his membership in the human family. He's a brother. God has become one of us. The dwelling place of God is with men. We now can call him "God-is-with-us." And we can no longer deal with God without dealing with our brother.

Because he first loved us, we ourselves are practicing love. If someone says, "I love God" (and even sets it to music and makes an anthem of it) *—if someone says, "I love God," and is hating his brother, he is a phony. For the man who has no love for his physical brother cannot possibly have love for the invisible God.*

So the advice we get from him is that the God-lover is also a brother-lover. Just a way of saying that from here on out, you can't have any dealings with God unless you deal with your fellow man, for God has established residency on the earth.

Now, this body (the Church) has been impregnated. The baby has been born. It's growing up now and it's learning how to talk. It's going out into the world and starting a little talking and a little acting and it's doing the same thing that it did when it was born of the one woman, Mary. This new Jesus—this new body of his—is still engaged in his old work. So we read in Acts, chapter 9:

Now one afternoon, about three o'clock, Rock and Jack were going into the church to pray. There was this guy who was born a cripple and who was put every day at the main entrance of the sanctuary to panhandle from those going to church.

That was the place where all the dignified people went in. That was the choice begging spot. This guy knew it. And he was at the main entrance to the sanctuary and he knew the best time to panhandle was when folks were on the way to Church, not after they came out. Now, I cannot believe that this panhandler was sitting there for forty years begging in the choicest spot the Church could offer (for begging) without some previous arrangement with the church officials. I think that perhaps he had worked out a concession with Caiaphas the high priest and Annas, the associate minister, and with the Sanhedrin, the official board. And I think the concession perhaps consisted of 10 per cent of the rake-off. All of which, of course, would go to missions.

Now, I think this beggar had a real stake there. He had been there for forty years and it was to the advantage of the Church not to do anything about his condition. It was a profitable kind of thing. Many times it is much more profitable to leave a man lame, because you can always quote your statistics with him. If you cure him, he might jump up and go home. But if you leave him lame you can at least report to the denominational board the 10 per cent of the cut you got from his begging. And you can always report that you have got some integration there, even if you have only one beggar to prove it. So it was to the advantage of the Church not to heal this man.

When this fellow saw Rock and Jack about to go in, he started putting the bite on them. Rock, with Jack backing him up, looked the fellow in the eye and said, "Look straight at us." And the beggar smiled big at them, thinking they were a soft touch. Then Rock said, "I don't have one thin dime, but I'm going to give you what I do have." (And I imagine at this point, the beggar kind of lost interest and said, "You go on in, buddy. I know how it is.")

"But," Rock said, "I do have something I want to give you. In the name of Jesus Christ of Nazareth, WALK." And grabbing him by the right hand, Rock pulled him to his feet. (Rock wasn't going to wait for that fellow to obey, Rock was going to give him a little ministerial urge in the right direction. So he grabs him by the hand and picks him up and puts him on his feet.) *And instantly he got strength in his feet and ankles and started jumping around, and walking all over the place. He went with them into the church, walking and jumping and shouting God's praises.*

Imagine that! A beggar who's supposed to stay on the outside of the Church coming in. I imagine that they had just gotten to the morning anthem. They're singing "Gloria in excelsis Deo" and this guy is dancing up and down the aisle to the tune of it. It's disconcerting to any Church for a man to get that much religion in the sanctuary. And here he is, dancing up and down, and then there he is, standing in the aisle, just when the deacons are getting ready to take up the collection. I imagine he says, "Give me one of those plates; I got experience." And he starts taking up the collection! And, that's disturbing to a Church that was founded in 1793 and hasn't had a new idea in it since.

Everybody recognized him as the panhandler at the main entrance to the church and they were utterly amazed and astounded at what was happening to him. And while he was still hanging on to Rock and Jack, the whole congregation gathered around him in the vestibule. And when Rock saw what was happening, he said to them all, "My fellow church members, why are you so surprised at this? Or why are you staring at us as though this man has been made to walk by our own power or saintliness?"

Now, if we had been Rock we would have said, "Yes, sir, I thank you." Congratulations, Rock, for making that man whole. "Thank you, ma'am. It was a little bit difficult but I grabbed him by the hand and got him up. I'm going to report him to the next meeting. You know, I'm going to have him over there to give his testimony about how I raised him to his feet. In fact, since I've been pastor of this church I've put twenty-five people on their feet. And under the water . . . and various other things too. Yeah I . . ." Instead, Rock said, "Look, I didn't do it. We didn't do that. We didn't do it by our power." And then he said something truly amazing. He said:

"The God of Abraham, Isaac and Jacob, the God of our fathers, has exalted his boy, Jesus, whom you all framed and disowned before the governor, having decided that he should be killed. But you disowned the Special One, the Just One, and asked that a convicted murderer be made your leader. While indeed you assassinated life's noblest one, God raised him from the dead, of which fact we all are the evidence!"

Now this was the very clue to all of the New Testament preaching: that God had raised Jesus from the dead and we are the evidence of the resurrection. You know, on Easter Day all of us get prettified and we get on our nice garments and we get our flowers and perfume and we talk about Jesus being raised from the dead and how he's going to take us all to heaven one of these days. . . .

Well, that might be nice, but that isn't what the resurrection of Jesus is all about. God didn't raise Jesus from the dead to prove that he could raise a few cantankerous saints. He could do that. Man's belief in his own immortality has been very persistent, not only in the Christian religion but outside of it. God raised Jesus from the dead for a different purpose. When Jesus came in his first body men didn't like God around. It was a bad place for God to be. Sort of like having a preacher in the barbershop. And we felt uncomfortable with him here. And so we had to get rid of him. And we nailed him to the cross and said, "You go back home, God. Don't you mess around down here. We have to watch our language too much with you around. And we have to watch our ledger accounts too much when you're looking over our shoulder. And we have to be too careful on Saturday night when we're hitting the bottle rather heavy. Now you . . . God, you go back home . . . where you belong and be a good God, and we'll see you at eleven o'clock on Sunday morning."

By raising Jesus from the dead, God is refusing to take man's "No" for an answer. He's saying, "You can kill my boy if you wish, but I'm going to raise him from the dead, and put him right smack dab down there on earth again!" It's God saying, "I'm not going to take man's 'No' for an answer. I'm going to raise him up, plant his feet on the earth, and put him to preaching, teaching and healing again."

So the resurrection of Jesus was simply God's unwillingness to take our No for an answer. He raised Jesus, not as an invitation to us to come to heaven when we die, but as a declaration that He Himself has now established permanent, eternal residence on earth. The resurrection places Jesus on *this* side of the grave— here and now—in the midst of this life. He is not standing on the shore of eternity beckoning us to join him there. He is standing beside us, strengthening us in this life. The good news of the resurrection of Jesus is not that we shall die and go home with him, but that he has risen and comes home with us, bringing all his hungry, naked, thirsty, sick, prisoner brothers with him.

And we say, "Jesus, we'd be glad to have you, but all these motley brothers of yours, you had better send them home. You come in and we'll have some fried chicken. But you get your sick, naked, cold brothers out of here. We don't want them getting our new rug all messed up."

The resurrection is simply God's way of saying to man, "You might reject me if you will, but I'm going to have the last word.

I'm going to put my son right down there in the midst of you and he's going to dwell among you from here on out."

On the morning of the resurrection, God put life in the present tense, not in the future. He gave us not a promise but a presence. Not a hope for the future but power for the present. Not so much the assurance that we shall live someday but that he is risen today. Jesus' resurrection is not to convince the incredulous nor to reassure the fearful, but to enkindle the believers. The proof that God raised Jesus from the dead is not the empty tomb, but the full hearts of his transformed disciples. The crowning evidence that he lives is not a vacant grave, but a spirit-filled fellowship. Not a rolled-away stone, but a carried-away church.

These disciples all the way through are saying, not that he is risen because the grave is empty, but "He is risen because we're full. We are the evidence of the resurrection. He is risen not because the dead rise, but because we are alive. And we're doing the same things that he has taught us to do."

So then they asked Rock, "Again, what shall we do," and he said, *"My brothers, reshape your lives, and turn around so that the slate can be wiped clean of your past misdeeds and that opportunity for renewal might come to you from the lord. That he might send to you Jesus, his previously chosen leader."*

Rock is saying that the thrust of the resurrection of Jesus is the reshaping of the lives of the believers to conform to his life, the reshaping of their minds to conform to his mind, the reshaping of their style of life to conform to his style of life. But you know it's so hard to reshape our lives to conform with the Gospel. It's so much easier to reshape the Gospel to conform to our lives.

I just got a real beautiful, slick advertisement in the mail a while back. It's put out by a publishing company of religious books and records. It says, "This is your personal invitation to set sail on a Christian voyage of self-discovery in the company of three great Christian leaders." And when you open it up, you find that you can get an inside berth for $360 that week. But that's where the poor folks sleep. The really elite who are going to discover themselves sleep on the A deck in a deluxe outside room at $630 for the week.

"Where could you find a better place for Christian self-discovery than in the comfortable, congenial atmosphere of an ocean liner?" Where can you find a better place to find Christ than in the congenial, comfortable atmosphere of an ocean liner? That's easy to answer—anywhere! If these people want to know where to make a self-discovery, let them walk down the streets of Calcutta. Let them go to the market in Kinshasa. Let them go to Accra, Ghana. Let them go to any ghetto in America or any little country shack in rural America.

But you can't discover Christ in those places. You got to have more congenial circumstances.

"There's something about sea travel that breaks down the conventional barriers between people, and makes it possible for them to discuss spiritual matters with frankness, spontaneity, and informality."

And here I am—old-fashioned, fundamentalist me—unaware that sea travel breaks down the middle wall of partition. I was always under the impression that it was the sacrifice of Jesus Christ hanging on a cross that broke down the middle wall of partition and abolished the enmity. And now I'm learning in this modern time that it wasn't Jesus on a cross, it was a bunch of Christians on a cruiser.

"You'll be refreshed and renewed by the many vacation pleasures the trip has to offer. The luxury of shipboard living aboard the M.S. ——, basking in the warmth of the Caribbean sun, swimming in the ship's pool, enjoying concerts, entertainment, Christian movies, and community singing."

I'm going to try to get a note off to St. Paul to the effect that he got on the wrong boat going to Rome.

Now this is the clincher, this is the sales pitch:

"There is nothing newer, more modern, or more magnificent for your cruise to Nassau and Jamaica than the M.S. —— which was selected and chartered because it's the perfect setting for a meaningful, spiritual experience in today's world of jet aircraft, trips to the moon, and other technological achievements."

So, having substituted sea water for blood, a luxury cruiser for a cross, pleasure for pain, excitement for salvation, and a $630 berth for spiritual rebirth—having done all that, we have not reshaped our lives to conform to the Gospel. We've made a paltry little attempt with three paid inspirers to reshape the Gospel to fit into our materialistic way of life.

We had better listen to our brother of old when he says:

Reshape your lives and turn around so that the slate can be wiped clean.

INCARNATIONAL EVANGELISM

I do not think there was really but one method of New Testament evangelism. Let's look in the first chapter of the Gospel of John.

To begin with there was the idea. . . . I'm translating this word *logos* as "idea" instead of "word." A word is simply an expression which conveys an idea and the basic thing in a word is the idea.

To begin with, there was the idea, and it was a divine idea, for it was God's idea. This started off with God from the very beginning; everything has happened because of it, and apart from it, nothing of significance has ever occurred. In it was life, and the life was the light of society. And the light is still shining in the darkness and the darkness just couldn't put it out.

Now, there was a man who'd been sent from God whose name was John. This man came to bear witness; this was his evangelism: to make known the great message. He came that he might have the testimony, that he might bear witness about the light so that all might believe through him. He was not the light, but he was just testifying about the light.

There was the true light which illuminates every human being coming into the world, and it was in the world and the world was made because of it. And yet the world ignored it. He came into those things which were his own and those people who were his own passed him by. But as many as did catch on, he gave to them the authority to become God's children—that is, all of those who really trusted in his name who were sired not out of blood of pagan altars nor out of the lust of human flesh nor were they sired out of the legitimate bonds of matrimony, but out of God's activity.

So then, the idea became a human and He lived among us."

The word here is *eskēnōsen,* which means "a tent." "He pitched his tent among us." Tents were actually living places, mobile homes, in those days. We might even say:

And so, the idea became a human and parked his trailer next to ours. And we all examined his credentials, credentials such as an only son receives from a father who's full of grace and truth. John evangelized, bore the message about him, and cried out saying, "This is the one about whom I was talking when I said, 'He who comes after me has become ahead of me, because He's my boss.'" Now, we all have received from his abundance one favor after another. The law was turned over to us by Moses, but grace and *truth came through Jesus Christ. Nobody at any time has ever set their eyes on God. The only or unique Son, who is from the bosom of the Father, that one has made him crystal clear."*

So far as I can determine, the only method of evangelization is that of incarnation. This is how God himself evangelized the world. He made other attempts. The Old Testament method of evangelism was that of revelation from Sinai. There, God came down to earth in the thunder and the lightning and the smoking of the mountain; and God spoke to his deputy and wrote his message for mankind on tables of stone. But the writer of the Hebrews says that God was a little disappointed in that evangelistic method, so he was going to tear up the old covenant and go write a new one. He was going to try a new approach to mankind. The writer of the Hebrews says that this time when he wrote, it was not tables of stone, but a man. God has made his good news, his idea, known to mankind by becoming a man. In Christ, God confronted the world with his visible word.

I think God had come to realize that even though he had made mankind with ears, man could no longer hear. Today, men cannot hear. They are stone deaf. But man's losing his ears sharpened his eyesight so that, while he cannot hear, he sure can see.

I had this to face many years ago when we went to Koinonia. The little country church to which I belonged invited me one summer to hold a revival meeting. They had heard I had graduated from the Baptist Theological Cemetery—uh, Seminary. So I accepted, and I preached to those people and I preached the word of God in *south Georgia,* and I didn't think that I would survive the ordeal, for when Jesus went back to his little home town to preach not a revival but just one youth sermon on Sunday morning they caught on to what he was saying before he even got to his closing point, and they took him out to the end of town to dash him over the hill. (That's one of the big troubles about Jesus' preaching: you can understand it.) Well, I expected to be in that dilemma, but I wasn't; much to my amazement, when I got through preaching, these dear ole deacons came by and said, "That was a *sweet* talk." And I wondered where they were during that sermon! They again asked me to preach and again I tried to make it clear. I supplied for the pastor time and again but somehow I could never make myself heard. But gradually, as Koinonia took shape and the word that had been preached to these people became flesh and they could see it, then they caught on. Not only was I not asked to preach to those people anymore, I was excommunicated, along with all the rest at Koinonia, from the membership of that church. At last, the sermon had been delivered. Men can see, but men find it difficult to hear.

So the method of evangelization of the New Testament is to confront men with a visible word. Now, if we were writing the account of the incarnation today, perhaps it would run something like this: "The word became a sermon and was later expanded into a book and the book sold well and inspired other books until of the making of books there was no end. And the world died in darkness and was buried in the theological library."

John—supposedly the same John, writing years later—says in the opening of his first letter:

That which was from the beginning, which we have heard, which we have looked on with our eyes, which we have gazed on and which our hands have handled about the idea of life. Now the life became crystal clear and we all looked at it and we are testifying and we are evangelizing you with the eternal light which was from the Father and which has been made real to us, which we have looked on and listened to—with this we are evangelizing you so that you all might have partnership with us all. Our partnership is with the Father and with his Son, Jesus Christ. We are writing things like this to you so that your joy may be complete. And this is the evangel which we heard from him and with which we now evangelize you: that God, indeed, is light, and there isn't any darkness at all in him. If we say that we have a partnership with him and then we keep on walking in the dark, we are telling a lie and are not doing the truth. But if we keep on walking in the light as he is in the light, we have partnership with him and the blood of Jesus, his Son, cleans us of all our sin. Now, if we say, "We haven't got any sin," we are kidding ourselves and the truth is not in us. But if we confess our sins, he is indeed faithful and just and will forgive us our sins and cleanse us of our wickedness. If we say we have not sinned, we are telling a lie, we are making a liar out of him, and his idea is not a reality in our midst.

I don't know how he could make it any more clear that the method of evangelization is confronting the world with an accomplished fact—that which *is*. "That which has taken place among us, we declare unto you." I don't think we have a right to bear witness to that which we do not experience. The incarnation, then, is the announcement of the Good News as fact.

I was at a Negro girls' college in Atlanta a few days ago for Religious Emphasis Week. There was a young girl from Africa— an exchange student—and during one of the dormitory sessions in which I was trying to bear testimony to some of the Christian truths, she rose and asked if she could say a word. This young woman from Africa fixed her eyes on me and it seemed to me they glowed like the eyes of a tiger at midnight. She looked me in the face and she said to me through clenched teeth, "How *dare* you send missionaries to Africa!" She had been experiencing some "Christian" treatment in Atlanta, Georgia, by people who were sending missionaries to Africa to bring the light to the people of Africa. And she fastened those eyes on me and said, "How *dare* you!"

How can you evangelize except from the standpoint of the incarnation? How can you go and say to people, "That which we would like to know—that declare we unto you. That which is not a reality among us, we declare unto you—a brotherhood which we cannot practice." How *dare* we preach, how *dare* we evangelize, from any standpoint except that of the incarnation!

The incarnation is not what Greek grammar calls the "punctiliar action." There are two kinds of action in the Greek verb. One is called "punctiliar action," action which is represented as a point—here and it's over. And then there is what is called "linear action" which represents the actions in the verb as continuing. The incarnation is not "punctiliar action." It is not a point in history in which God invaded the earth and returned; it is an invasion which is continuing.

This incarnation evangelism is total. It must embrace the whole man. It must not save his soul at the expense of his body nor his body at the expense of his soul. An evangelism which does not cover the totality of human experience is emasculated and deformed. The Word became not a crippled man but man's most perfect man with every member of his body entire and complete. The incarnation, then, must reach to the tiniest extremity of our limbs. It must reach to the unnumbered hairs on our head and to every part of our body and embrace the totality of human experience.

I would like to point out one instance in Jesus' ministry where he did this kind of evangelism. Reading from the eighth chapter of Luke beginning with the twenty-sixth verse:

So they sailed on over into the country of the Gerasenes, which is over across the sea from Galilee, and there came out to him in that land a certain man out of the city who had a demon and was for a long time not wearing clothing. And he was not living in a house but in the tombs and when he saw Jesus he cried out and fell down in front of him and with a loud voice he said, "What have you and I in common, Jesus, you Son of God most high? I beg you, don't torment me." Now Jesus was commanding the unclean spirit to come out of that man. For a long time, they had captured him and bound him with chains, and shackled him with foot fetters and he would rip off the chains and would be driven by the demon into the desolate places. And Jesus was asking him, "What's your name?" And he said, "Legion," because many devils had entered into him. And they were asking Jesus that he would not command them to go into the abyss. Now there was there a large herd of pigs (Matthew says there were 2,000 of them) *being fed on the hillside. And the demons begged him that he might allow them to go into the pigs and he allowed them and when they came out from the man they entered into the pigs and the whole herd rushed down the slope into the lake and were drowned. And when the herdsmen saw what had happened, they fled and announced it in the city and in the fields. Then they all went out to see what had happened and they came to Jesus and found the man from whom the devil had been cast sitting at his feet fully clothed and in his right mind and it just scared the daylights out of them. And they who had seen it all announced* (and here they were evangelists too, they were bearing the news) *how the demon man had been saved. And so the whole multitude of that surrounding—of the country of the Gerasenes—asked him to please go away from them because a great fear had seized them and he got into the boat and returned. Now the man from whom the devils had come out begged him to let him go with him but Jesus wouldn't allow it. He said, "You go on back home to your house and declare there what God has done for you." And he went away through the whole city preaching what God, what Jesus, had done for him.*

Now this is a strange story on the surface, but it's a story that all three Synoptic Gospels relate. You remember Jesus is tired. He's been evangelizing in Galilee and he says to the disciples, "Let's go over across the lake." They get in the boat, sail over across the sea of Galilee and as soon as they get out of the boat, this man comes to meet them. He's a man who has lived in the tombs. People have tried to chain him, they've tried to tame him. Jesus begins this encounter by asking him, "What is your name?" In other words, this man has got to become a human being again. These devils begin to enter into a conversation with Jesus and say, "Let us go into those hogs."

This, I think, will help you see how Jesus could not heal a man without perhaps dealing with the situation that produced his hurt. I think really we have here the source material on which Jesus built the story of the Prodigal Son in which a young boy went away into a far country and got a job feeding pigs. These hogs are the real point in this story. What are all these hogs doing right across the lake from Galilee, which is hog-dry? I think that, more than likely, these were bootleg hogs. What would a man be doing raising 2,000 hogs right across the lake from a hog-dry country if he wasn't curing those country hams and slipping them over to Galilee?

Those folks from the South, they were the fundamentalists who had been taught that you dare not eat hog meat. But the northerners, the liberals up in Galilee, had become more liberalized on hog meat and they would at least lap up a little red-eye gravy occasionally. Down in the Deep South, in the Bible Belt, you didn't jump over the line like that. I think this demon-possessed man from Judea had been brought up in a devout home and had been taught it was wrong to eat hog meat. But now, in this far-off country, he begins to be in want and he's got nothing to eat and he goes out and gets a job, of all things, feeding hogs. You can imagine the tension in that man's heart as he goes about feeding these hogs, which his mama and daddy had taught him were the worst things on the face of the earth—"unclean, unclean!"—and here he was feeding them.

I know the tension in the heart of a man caught in this kind of thing. I've been in it myself. And I've seen it time and again. A fellow came to Koinonia recently who had come out of World War II shell-shocked. At night he would get up sometimes and walk and as he walked he would rip his clothes until he had not a thread on him.

One night the sheriff called us and said he had him in town. He said the man was naked and he had charged him with indecency and had him in jail. We finally got him out and I tried to find out why a man would do that. One day he was talking to me and he said, "You know, I was brought up in North Carolina, and I had very godly parents. They taught me not to kill, but to love people. I couldn't even kill a sparrow. I wouldn't even go hunting. And then the war came along and they drafted me and they put a gun in my hand and they sent me overseas and I shot and killed a man." When he said that he pulled his clothes and popped a button, and I realized that maybe his clothes represented guilt. He wanted to get it off himself. He wanted to be free of this terrible division of being a follower of God but having to practice an evil thing. It's an awful thing to teach a child the gospel of Jesus Christ if you do not intend to make it real for him. This man would have been much better off if he had never heard the gospel of Jesus. Here he was broken and torn.

This is the situation for the young fellow in the story. He was in a bootleg situation, feeling that what he was doing was wrong, so that Jesus could not restore to that man any measure of sanity until he got rid of those hogs. In dealing with the hogs, Jesus was dealing with the most difficult element in the situation. He was dealing with the power structure that owned those hogs. When those 2,000 high-priced black-market hogs went into the sea it was a considerable loss. The people came out to Jesus and found this man, now not bound by chains but sitting in his right mind—in the mind he should have had all along—sitting at the feet of Jesus, fully clothed.

Now this is way out on the farm. Where did these clothes come from? Where did this guy get the clothes that he had on his back? I don't know but I would guess it went something like this: "Hey, Rock. Come here. What size shirt you wear?" "16½." "All right, Rock, let's have it. Andy. What size britches you wear?" "I wear a 32-34." "That's about right. Let's have 'em." I imagine that little bunch of disciples gathered around this man and clothed him.

Here is an evangelism that tackles the worst of social problems and the worst of spiritual problems. It does not stop until it has not only healed a man and saved his soul, but has gotten rid of the very thing that produced his despair, and then gathered the fellowship around him and clothed him with their own clothes.

This is real New Testament evangelism. But then it doesn't stop there. This guy says, "I want to go with you." Jesus said, "No, son, you know your old daddy, just before I left Judea he was telling me about you. He said: 'You know, I have two fine boys. One of them's still with me; he's helping me on the farm. But one of them, the younger one, I don't know what happened to him. He got it in his head he wanted to leave and I gave him money and he left and I haven't had as much as a postcard from him. Jesus, you travel around a good bit; if you should run across him, tell him his old pappy loves him and would like to have him home any time he wants to come.' "

This boy said, "Let me go along with you." But Jesus said, "No, son. You go on back home." And when he got home, he was in his right mind.

Here is evangelism at its highest, based not upon a sermon, not upon a theory, not upon an abstraction, but upon the Word of God become flesh and dealing with us—with us demoniacs—and restoring us to our right minds.

II

The Substance
of Faith

*"Fear is the polio of the soul which
prevents our walking by faith."*

THE SUBSTANCE OF FAITH

I would like to read from the letter to the Hebrews—or more accurately, the sermon to the Hebrews. I shall begin with the first verse of the third chapter.

So then, committed brothers, partners in the spiritual assignment, give careful consideration to Jesus, the founder and leader of our movement; for he was loyal to the One who appointed him just as Moses was a loyal leader of his people. But Jesus is as much greater than Moses as the architect is greater than the house he designs. While every house is designed by someone, God alone is the master architect. Now Moses was indeed a trustworthy leader of his people as God's deputy, a symbol of the things to be discussed later. On the other hand, Christ leads his people not as the king's deputy but as his own son, and we Christians are his people —provided, of course, that we diligently carry through on our commitment and pledge of hope to the very last detail. It's just like the Holy Spirit says: "If you would take him seriously today, don't rationalize like they did that day in the wilderness when I got sick and tired of their demands for proof, when your fathers tried my patience with their let's-be-practical speeches and were given forty years in which to see plenty of my 'proof'. So I got thoroughly fed up with that bunch and I said they are eternally making a mess of things, simply because they pay no attention to my instructions. While in this upset condition, I swore that they would never arrive at my destination."

The author is referring to that time when the children of Israel were right out on the brink of the Promised Land. God, with mighty power, had led them out of the land of Egypt. He had given them a capable leader. He had given them food. When they got to hungering for their cucumbers and garlic, God gave them "manna." "Manna" is the Hebrew word for "what is it?" I'm sure that a lot of us have eaten "manna." Time and again, these folks went out there early in the morning and there was that bread stuff all over the ground like dew and they said, "What is it?" They had "what is it" every morning, noon, and night with crackle, crunch, and crinkle—every way you can fix it, they had this manna. But God had provided for their needs and he had told them he had a land for them and he got them ready to go into it. He said, "It's your land, folks. Go on in and take possession."

Well, like good brethren, they appointed a study commission and they decided they had better send some brethren in to look the land over. You know, we don't ever do anything in a hasty way. We've got to be careful and practical. So they were very democratic about it. They asked each tribe to choose one representative and they got twelve delegates and sent them to the annual conven—— I mean, sent them over into the land to look it over. Well, they went over and they were quite impressed by what they saw and they came back and made their report to the people. Ten of the brethren were very much impressed. They said, "We saw a land just flowing with milk and honey and the grapes were so big that it took two men to carry one bunch!"

Now, that was a ministerial estimate, I'm quite sure. And I think it's right there that they made the mistake, because when their eyes began to be distorted by the material things they saw, they were absolutely blinded, from that point on, to the spiritual things. In the first place, I think they slipped up on that land flowing with milk and honey. I've had experience in the production of both and I've never yet gotten milk from an artesian cow, nor have I gotten honey from bees that didn't have stingers. They slipped up by fastening their eyes on the material aspect of the country.

So, these people came back and gave their report and said they had found it a wonderful land, full of milk, honey, and big bunches of grapes. That got everybody enthused, and they were about ready to make a mass demonstration and move right on in when they said, "But there's one little hitch. There are giants in the land so big that we were as grasshoppers in their sight." Now, you see how their vision was distorted? I imagine the giants really weren't but five or six inches taller than they were, but the honey and the milk and the grapes had gotten them so blinded that giants were out of proportion too. And they said, "These giants were so big, we were just like grasshoppers." The ten fellows said, "We like that honey and we like that milk and we like those grapes. But hm-m-m-m, those giants!"

Well, Caleb and Joshua said, "It is a good land. It is flowing with milk and honey. It does have good grape possibilities. And there are giants. But," they said, "God has said it's our land. Now, let's go on in and take it."

Well, that was the minority report, and being good democratic people they accepted the majority report and decided to postpone this venture a little while until they could solve the giant problem. And God became angry and he said, "I got so upset with those people that I swore they would never get into my Promised Land because I told them to go in and they wouldn't take me seriously."

That's what this writer's talking about here. He said God had a lot of good things for them, but they wouldn't take him seriously and so God said, "While in this upset condition, I swore that they would never arrive at my destination."

Take extreme care, brethren, to see that not a one of you might have such a wicked and untrustful attitude as to turn your backs on the living God. Rather, remind each other every day during this period we call today, or the present, not to let one's soul get calloused by flimsy excuses. For we are Christ's partners only if we steadfastly carry through on our commitment from beginning to end, just like it says. I repeat, If you will take him seriously today, don't let your souls get calloused like they did that time they provoked him in the wilderness. Let me ask you, my brothers, who were the ones who were still stubborn even after they heard the full report? Wasn't it practically the whole gang that came out of Egypt under Moses? And with whom did God get fed up for those forty years? Wasn't it with those who missed the mark and who died like flies in the wilderness? And wasn't it to those who disobeyed that he swore that they would never arrive at his destination? So it is perfectly obvious that it was absence of faith which kept them from making the grade. Therefore, it should really frighten us to realize that we, like them, are given an opportunity to enter his Promised Land with the same possibility that some of us might flub the dub. For we have had the news to fall on our ears the same as they. The reason it didn't do them one bit of good was because their hearing and their faith didn't connect.

Now, these are some rather plain words and they're not mine. They're Mr. Hebrew's—I mean Mr. Whoever-Wrote-the-Hebrews —words. That's plain talk. He said the trouble with those people back there and the thing that stirred God's anger was not that they didn't understand, but that they professed a faith upon which they were unwilling to act.

Now, while love is the greatest of the abiding things mentioned by Paul when he speaks of faith, hope and love as abiding—while the greatest of these, I admit, is love—the scarcest of these is faith. Though we like to carry around a pocketful of coins on which is inscribed, "In God We Trust," we actually put our faith more in the material upon which this is inscribed than in the God to whom it pays tribute. And while we are embarrassed by surpluses of cotton, corn, peanuts, potatoes, autos, freezers, and TV's, there is no evidence of an oversupply of faith. It was so scarce in Jesus' day that he cried out, "When the son of man cometh, will He find faith on the earth? An amount so small as a mustard seed," he said, "could move mountains."

What is this faith? Let me tell you that faith is not a theoretical belief. I would go further and say that faith is not a stubborn belief in spite of all evidence. That is not faith. That is folly. I realize that there are many things which cannot be provable, for which there cannot be given evidence from a scientific standpoint. All the great things of the Spirit cannot be supported by scientific evidence. That does not mean that they're lacking in evidence. It means that they're lacking in that particular approach to evidence. We do not demand evidence along the lines of the Spirit. Those are things for which we dare not ask proof. And yet, to stubbornly hold to an idea when all of the evidence points the other way need not be interpreted as faith.

Down our way, for many years when I was a kid growing up, I was familiar with a cult of people called "snake handlers" and they would handle those big rattlesnakes at their meeting and whether or not you had faith was whether or not you would handle the snakes. I never reached that state of spiritual maturity. But some people did and some people got bit by the snakes. They were told by the reverend that if they got bit and had enough faith, they wouldn't die. Well, there were some so obviously lacking in faith that they had a number of funerals. But it was not faith that these people had; it was folly.

Faith is not belief in spite of evidence. Somewhat like the dear soul who had a big hill right out the back window that obstructed her view and she wanted it moved awfully bad. One day she read in the Bible where it says if you have faith even as a grain of mustard, you can say to this mountain, "Be uprooted" and it will be dashed into the sea. And she says, "I got it." So that night she prayed that the hill would be cast into this little pond down the way. She jumped up bright and early the next morning and looked out the window and there the hill was. She said, "I knew it. I knew it. I knew it would still be there!"

Well, that is not faith. That is foolishness. Faith is not belief in spite of evidence but a life in scorn of the consequences.

Now, faith and belief in the New Testament are interchangeable. The same Greek word which is sometimes translated "belief" is another time translated "faith." We have come to dissociate belief from faith and we think of belief as a way of thinking when the original intent was not to describe a way of thinking but a way of acting. Actually, our English word *be-lief* comes from the old Anglo-Saxon *be,* which means "by," and *lief,* which means "life." What one lives by is actually his belief or his by-life. This is the New Testament meaning of belief and faith. It is what you live by, it is the kind of life which you live. Now, in Hebrews 11:1 the author gives a definition of this kind of faith of which he's speaking. He says:

"Faith is the activation of our aspirations, the life based on unseen realities. It is conviction translated into deeds. In short, it is the word become flesh." So as long as the word remains a theory to us, and is not incarnated by our actions and translated by our deeds into a living experience, it is not faith. It may be theology, but it is not faith. Faith is a combination of both conviction and action. It cannot be either by itself.

To give you one illustration, a number of years ago, I was invited by a Southern Baptist church in North Carolina to come and speak. I looked the place up on the map and found that it was a little suburb of a big city in North Carolina and I figured that it was some swank, aristocratic, liberal church that wanted somebody to come to it and pat it on the back for its liberal views toward race. So I figured that I'd get me up a sermon and I'd hold those folks over the brink and singe their eyebrows. I wanted a chance to really preach to a Southern Baptist church because I hadn't had that chance since a Baptist church had turned me out five years previously. There was just a little bit of revenge, I guess.

I went over there and instead of it being a big swank suburban church, it was a little mill-town church that was on the edge of the city and the city had grown up and engulfed it. The church would seat about 300 and I think they had about 600 in it. The thing that amazed me was that these people were white and Negro just sitting anywhere they wanted to sit. And back of me was a choir with about 50 voices in it and over half of them were Negroes. Well, I had to change my subject. When I got through, the pastor got up and he said, "Now, we're going to have dinner on the grounds." I really trembled then, because it's one thing for black and white folks to worship together; it's another thing for them to eat together. Here the man was advocating social equality right there in the South.

The choir got up and sang, "Let us Break Bread Together on Our Knees," and we went out and I thought sure these folks would go out to the back yard of the church, but they went out on the front yard and spread their tables right out on the main street of this little town, and started eating together. When they started eating together and talking together, I knew this wasn't an unusual thing. I knew they had been doing this a long time.

I went over to the pastor, and I said, "You know, this is a rather amazing thing to me. Were you integrated before the Supreme Court decision?"

He said, "What decision?"

He explained: "Well, back during the depression, I was a worker here in this little mill. I didn't have any education. I couldn't even read and write. I got somebody to read the Bible to me, and I was moved and I gave my heart to the Lord, and later, I felt the call of the Lord to preach.

"This little church here was too poor to have a preacher and I just volunteered. They accepted me and I started preaching. Someone read to me in there where God is no respecter of persons, and I preached that."

I said, "Yeah. How did you get along?"

"Well," he said, "the deacons came around to me after that sermon and said, 'Now, brother pastor, we not only don't let a nigger spend the night in this town, we don't even let him pass through. Now, we don't want that kind of preaching you're giving us.'"

I said, "What did you do?"

"Well," he said, "I fired them deacons."

"How come they didn't fire you?"

"Well," he said, "they never had hired me. I just volunteered."

"Did you have any more trouble with them?"

"Yeah. They came back at me again."

"What did you do with them that time?"

"I turned them out. I told them anybody that didn't know any more about the gospel of Jesus than that not only shouldn't be an officer in the church, he shouldn't be a member of it. I had to put them out."

I said, "Did you have to put anybody else out?"

"Well, I preached awfully hard, and I finally preached them down to two. But," he said, "those two were committed. I made sure that any time after that, anybody who came into my church understood that they were giving their life to Jesus Christ and they were going to have to be serious about it. What you see here is a result of that."

I thank God there was still one unruined preacher in the South who had no better sense than to preach the gospel. Maybe it was fortunate that some of our educators didn't get hold of him. Now, I don't mean to be putting emphasis upon the man's ignorance. I don't think that made any difference. I think it was the man's *faith* that brought the power to his church. He was willing to couple a conviction with a way of action and take the consequences.

Why, then, is it so difficult to have faith? Why is faith so scarce? I think the clue to this is simply fear. Faith and fear, like light and darkness, are incompatible. Fear is the polio of the soul which prevents our walking by faith. The children of Israel gave as their excuse giants in the land. Here, we see the long tentacles of fear creeping out and laying their cold clammy hands upon the people and blinding them to the express command of God.

No doubt these children of Israel tried to justify their fears by having study courses on giants. I imagine that they went to the library and got an encyclopedia down and looked up "giants, species of, life histories of, emotional habits of, effects of giants' heels on grasshoppers." And I think, as a result of that study, they came to the conclusion that they had to be practical. This was a serious matter, and they would have to map out some strategy. So they appointed a social action committee to map the strategy. They came up with the recommendation that they invade this new land with leaflets and that they put on a "Be Kind to Grasshoppers" week. Then, of course, they had to have a finance committee to raise funds for the "Be Kind to Grasshoppers" week, and for the relief of widows of squished grasshoppers.

Now, all their study, all their enlightenment, all their activity was *nothing* because it was not coupled with faith in the God who had told them, "Go on in, it's yours."

The purpose and function of fear is self-preservation. Its danger is when it performs its function too well, like an overactive gland. Fear's ultimate enemy is death, and fear can be brought under control only when it is convinced that this archenemy has been abolished. The purpose of fear in our lives is to preserve us and keep us alive. Fear is very active and it's a very good thing and it works in us and tries its best to keep us alive and it fights with all it's got against this archenemy, death.

We cannot have faith until we understand this aspect of fear—that fear will be overactive in us so long as it sees, anywhere on the horizon, the specter of death. If we are going to be triumphant over fear, we must have an assurance of triumph over death. The clue, then, to the triumphant faith of the early Christians lies in the power of the resurrection. They did not go everywhere preaching the ethics of Jesus. They went everywhere preaching that this Jesus whom you slew, God has raised him from the dead. Death had lost its sting, the grave had lost its victory. Fear no longer was overactive in them, and they could go everywhere, saying, "We must obey God rather than men. Kill this old body if you will. Let goods and kindred go, this mortal life also." It was when Christ raised triumphant over death that fear could be put back into its proper place and faith could shine forth radiantly and powerfully.

The life, the crucifixion, and the resurrection of Jesus is one package. I think the weakness of liberalism today is that it accepts the life of Jesus, but shuns the inevitable consequences of the Jesus Life, which is crucifixion, and is thereby denied the power of the resurrection. When we are given assurance that this Jesus and the kind of life that he lived cannot be put out, that the light is still shining in the darkness and the darkness can not overcome it, then we are freed from our fear. Then we can give ourselves to this God and say, "Let *all* that we have go, even this mortal life also."

THE ADVENTURES OF THREE STUDENTS IN A FIERY FURNACE

The adventures of three students in a fiery furnace is told in the Book of Daniel. This book, in point of time, was written perhaps closer to the New Testament than any other of the Old Testament books. Most scholars agree that it was written about 167 B.C. If this is true, it was written at a time of great persecution. On the throne was an emperor who called himself Antiochus Epiphanes. The Greek word *epiphanes* means "illustrious"—Antiochus the Illustrious. But so terrible were his persecutions, so bloodthirsty was this king that his subjects did not call him Epiphanes; they called him Epimines, which is Greek for "a man who's gone berserk," a fellow who is cuckoo. So this was written during the reign of an emperor who had gone cuckoo and it was written primarily to young people who were being forced against their will to obey government edicts to which they could not conscientiously agree.

The book, then, purports to be a treatise—at least the first six chapters of it—on what happens to a spiritually sensitive person when his government and his God are on a collision course. Now, since we today are facing more and more of this in the world, where governments are prone to assume the prerogatives of God, this book might become the most relevant of all of the Old Testament books. It is not a historical narrative. While the setting is in about 587 B.C. in the court of Nebuchadnezzar, everyone who read the book would know that the writer was not talking about King Nebuchadnezzar. He's talking about King Epiphanes. And everyone would know that Shadrach, Meshach, and Abednego, and Daniel are really not actual historical figures. They are people as real as Rhett Butler and Scarlett O'Hara in *Gone With the Wind*. This might be considered a historical parable in which the writer has concealed a truth; and the truth is that in the time of testing, when God and government are on collision course, God calls his people to be faithful to him even though it means disobedience to the government.

Now, let's take just one episode of the many in this book. The king had brought these three students over as foreign students, as international students, to go to school at Babylon. They were taken from south Geor—— uh, Judea and brought over into Babylon to be trained in all the wisdom of the Babylonians. And then, at the end of the three-year course, they were to be sent before the king. They already had their undergraduate work and they were now in the divinity school. And when they got through, they were to appear before the king to see whether they had the proper ministerial tone and etiquette. They had completed their ministerial training and, unfortunately, they had had some good teachers who had helped them to catch on to what God is all about. I think one of the worst things that a teacher can do in the seminary is to help his students understand what Christianity's all about. It gets them into all kinds of trouble. I think one of the worst things about Jesus' sermons was that you could understand them.

These three fellows had caught on to the fact that God was still alive and kicking around in the world and that he was the Lord of human history and that he was not to be tinkered and tampered with and that no professor, even though he had a Ph.D. and was teaching at a university, could bury God. Now, I want to take one episode that's in the third chapter of the Book of Daniel. This writer sets the stage. He says:

Nebuchadnezzar the king made an image of gold, whose height was threescore cubits and the breadth thereof was six cubits.

It's sixty by six. Now, we're not Hebrews, but the Hebrews would get a real bang out of this because numbers symbolized certain things to them. The number thirteen to us symbolizes un-luckiness. Many hotels don't have a thirteenth floor. Airplanes sometimes don't have Number Thirteen seats. To the Jews, the six meant incomplete, imperfect. Here's an image now that's sixty cubits high and six cubits wide, and to the Hebrew students this would mean that this is a blasphemous image. It's the acme of imperfection. The government had made a great mistake in ever embarking upon it.

He set it up in the plain of Dura, in the province of Babylon.

Now, the plain was out where the peasants work, where they toil in the fields and grow the corn, the cotton, the peanuts, and the tobacco, and all that kind of stuff. In other words, the king was setting up this golden image out there on the plains where he had extracted the taxes from these farmers. He had ground their faces to the earth and squeezed the blood out of them so that he could erect a mighty image of gold and he had the audacity to put it up out in front of the very people he had exploited. It would be about like levying a heavy tax on Negroes and then putting up a gold monument to Abraham Lincoln and locating it in Harlem. It would be blasphemy.

I think in all fairness we ought to say that this great golden image was not financed by the C.I.A. through an aid to the Baby-lonian Ministry of Worship. This was the real stuff. This guy had gotten it out of the people and he hadn't gotten it from any foreign aid. It was an image of gold. Now, I'm not sure who built it; he might have let the contract out to some of his allies. It could be that he might have let the contract out to some big American firms to build the head, the body, the legs, and maybe the local people got to contract for building the little finger on the left hand.

Now, Nebuchadnezzar was proud of this thing, and so he wanted to have a big dedication. The writer says:

Then Nebuchadnezzar the king sent to gather together the satraps, the deputies, the governors, the judges, the treasurers, the counsellors, the sheriffs, and all the rulers of the provinces.

I imagine the Imperial Lizard was invited and all the other folks; this was just a big to-do and the emperor invited them all to come to the dedication. Just prior to that, he might have had a $100-a-plate dinner for fund-raising to help defray some of the expenses of the image, and they were all going to have a big time at this dedication. They even had the Marine Band out there.

The satraps, the deputies, the governors, the judges, the treasurers, the counsellors, the sheriffs, and all the rulers of the provinces were gathered together unto the dedication of the image that Nebuchadnezzar the king had set up, and they stood before the image. Then the herald cried aloud (the herald—in those days, that was the equivalent of the Baptist preacher who opened the meeting with an invitation) —*the herald cried aloud, "To you it is commanded, O people, nations, and languages, that at what time ye hear the sound of the cornet, the flute, the harp, the sackbut, the psaltery, the dulcimer, and all kinds of music, you fall down and worship the golden image that Nebuchadnezzar the king has set up."*

Now, you would have thought that when the herald cried that everybody had to fall down on their face when they heard the first strain of "The Stars and Stripes Forever," that somebody would have objected. But all these bigwigs obediently bowed down and all fell on their face.

Because (Nebuchadnezzar says) *whoso falleth not down and worshippeth shall the same hour be cast into the midst of a burning fiery furnace.*

In those days, you didn't burn your draft card; you got burnt.

Therefore, at that time when all the people heard the sound of the cornet, the flute, the harp, the sackbut, the psaltery, and all kinds of music all the people and the nations and the languages fell down and worshipped the golden image that Nebuchadnezzar the king had set up.

I think in all fairness we ought also to say that the sackbut player had not infiltrated the royal orchestra to try to find out whether or not the dulcimer section was Communist. This was the real thing and they were there to pay homage to the king and they were to bow down in unison. The king had learned that to get real obedience out of the people, you had to have them marching to music, you had to have a big festive occasion, whip up the spirit of unity, and say, "We're not going to have any dissent." This seems to be a very pleasant occasion for the king. He's been elected by an overwhelming majority and it looks like his chances for re-election are pretty good, and he's quite happy that he's built this big image. Of course, he had to levy a 10 per cent surcharge, but other than that, he got by all right and everything looked fine and rosy.

But, then, there's always a fly in the ointment. These young theologs have a way of getting out of hand and some of them are going to kick over the traces if you aren't careful—and, sure enough, this is what happened.

Wherefore at that time certain Chaldeans came near and brought accusation against the Jews.

Now, I don't know who these Chaldeans were. My guess is that they were the ancient "John Besmirch Society" and that they were noticing that these Hebrews weren't quite 100 per cent loyal. They had studied the history of these Hebrews and found that these aliens who had been brought over there to Babylon at one time had been sojourners in Egypt—their great-great-great-great-great-great-grandfather had been a servant under Phara-ho, and it might have been that they still carried over some of those doctrines, you know. And these John Besmirchers were watching them very, very carefully.

And here's what they said: *They answered and said to King Nebuchadnezzar, "O King, live forever!"* (That's the ancient counterpart of "Heil, Hitler!") *"O King, live forever! We got some news for you."* Now, you would have thought at least they would have waited until the dedication was over to spoil the king's day. But they didn't. Right in the middle of the dedication service, they come whispering up there: "Hey, Nebuchadnezzar, we got some news for you. There're some folks that are not bowing down. There're some folks that didn't fall on their faces when the band struck up." And Nebuchadnezzar is just furious.

In his rage and fury he commanded to bring Shadrach, Meshach, and Abednego. And they brought these men before the king. Nebuchadnezzar spoke and said to them, "Is it a-purpose, O Shadrach, Meshach, and Abednego, that ye serve not my gods nor worship the golden image which I have set up?"

That's a lot of royal jargon for saying, "Bubba, did you do this on purpose? Did you know what you were doing? Didn't you hear what I ordered?" Then Nebuchadnezzar softens up a little bit, gets rather paternalistic and says:

"Now if ye be ready at what time ye hear the sound of the cornet, the flute, the harp, the sackbut, the psaltery, and the dulcimer. (King Nebuchadnezzar knew how many pieces there were in his orchestra.) *If then ye be ready, ye fall down and worship the image which I have made. But if ye worship not, ye shall be cast the same hour into the midst of a burning fiery furnace and who is that God that shall deliver you out of my hands?"*

He's saying, "Now, fellow, I hope you didn't do this on purpose. But in case you did, I'm going to get the band to start over with the 'Star-Spangled Banner' and if you're ready to give the loyalty oath at that moment, then we'll forgive you. But if not" —and then Nebuchadnezzar pulls his trump card out of his deck— "into the fiery furnace!"

That fiery furnace was the central heating system of the whole empire. That's what heated up everybody. All this hot patriotism was really not so much love for the country but fear of the furnace. Nebuchadnezzar offers these kids the prospect of doing one of two things: *1*) just simply falling down and worshipping before that image which would have been a relatively easy thing to do. They were already standing up there before it. All they had to do was fall down. Or *2*) take a little trip to the fiery furnace. Well, these kids answer in a way that I think is really superb. Here's what they say. I want to read their words.

Shadrach, Meshach, and Abednego answered and said to the king, "O Nebuchadnezzar, we have no need to answer thee in this matter. If it be so, our God whom we serve is able to deliver us from the burning fiery furnace; and he will deliver us out of your hand. But if not, be it known unto thee, O king, that we will not serve thy gods nor worship the golden image which thou hast set up."

They said, "O king, this God we serve is no foreign God. We know him quite well. And we are convinced that he is greater than you are and that he can deliver us out of your hands. We might be ashes, but he'll blow us out of your hand. You don't have the power to hold us. But even if he doesn't, we want you to know, O king, that we still aren't going to bow down to your image." Now, this took some real dedication, saying they believe that God will deliver them but even if he doesn't, they still aren't going to bow down. These young fellows were saying, "You know, if we've got to take our choice between living in a country where men are slaves or dying in a furnace where men are free, we choose the furnace. We had rather be ashes than asses." That's rather straight talk that even a king can understand. And the king gives the order, "Fire up the furnace. We got some stuff to go in it."

Now, with normal criminals like car thieves and dope addicts and bootleggers, you can run the furnace at normal temperature. But when you've got a civil disobedient guy on your hand, you've got to heat it up, 'cause this is no normal crime. You can even handle such crimes as murder at normal temperature. But when you get up to challenging the authority of the king himself, then the king can't deal with that kind of violation with just the furnace running along as usual. So he says to them, "Heat that thing up seven times hotter than it's ever been before."

Here again, there's a little bit of symbology in the numbers. The number six indicated incompleteness. The number seven indicated completeness. The week had seven days in it; the whole number of seven meant completeness. What Nebuchadnezzar's saying here is, "Open up every burner, even the afterburner, and get it as hot as it can possibly be heated." He orders that they be bound and they are thrown in. The fire is so hot, it says, that the guys that threw them in got killed by it. That's a hot fire.

Well, the night passed and the furnace began to cool down a little bit. By the time it got to where you could get within reasonable distance of it, Nebuchadnezzar decided he would go see whether these three young civil disobedient guys were properly cremated. So he goes out and looks in. And, to his amazement, he sees four men in there. He calls his men and says, "Looky here. Didn't we sentence three men? How is it that now I see four men and one I see in there is like unto the Son of God?" Nebuchadnezzar cries out, "Shadrach! Meshach! Abednego! Come forth and come hither!"

That was no time for civil disobedience, and Shadrach, Meshach, and Abednego obeyed the king, and they came out—all three of them. Three? I thought there were four. Where is the fourth one? The one like the Son of God—maybe he's still in there. Maybe he's waiting for more students named Shadrach, Meshach, and Abednego, so he can walk around with them in the fiery furnace; for he knows what a fiery furnace is like.

What then is this book saying to us? I think it says four things. First, that human institutions, whether they be political, ecclesiastical, or otherwise, are capable of gross error. The error is usually in proportion to the power and pride of the institution, whether it be ecclesiastical or political. Secondly, this book is saying that extreme attempts are made to produce total conformity to the error. We see this in the Roman empire when it was about to fall apart at the seams the emperor deified himself and set up emperor worship and commanded that there be no dissent. Thirdly, it is saying that God's call to obedience can be heard above the tumult, above the bands, and above the flag-waving. This means that his call may be costly and extremely dangerous.

Anyone who embarks on a course of obedience to God when his government is on collision course with God must be prepared for the fiery furnace. And fourthly, it says that God alone is ultimately the Lord of history, that he is greater than kings and their furnaces, as well as their gas chambers.

Are there any Shadrachs today? Are there any young students in the fiery furnace? Yes, I know of one. His name isn't Shadrach, his name is Tom Rodd. Tom Rodd is a young man nineteen years of age. He was eighteen a year ago when he felt that he could not conscientiously go into the draft system. He refused to register. He was brought up before a judge in Philadelphia and sentenced to four years. The judge probated the sentence on the grounds that Tom Rodd would not engage in any peace demonstrations of any kind. Tom began to serve his probated sentence; but then as the war in Vietnam became to Tom an increasingly immoral affair, he felt that he had to violate his terms of probation and participate in a peace demonstration. He was brought again before the judge, and I want to read you Tom's statement just prior to his resentencing. It's one of the most eloquent statements that I have heard from any man of any age in America. How a young fellow could make this kind of statement, I don't know. It must have been that he had been with Jesus.

Tom said, "Your Honor, one year and four months ago, you and I met each other in this building. What brought us together then was my conscientious refusal to co-operate with our government's draft system. You came as a representative of the government with the authority and the responsibility which that office implies. Now we are together again, and again you are here as a representative of the United States Government, this time because I have openly violated the special terms of probation that you set down the last time we met. I'm sorry that I have only known you in your official capacity. You and I are human beings; we are together, as brothers, wrapped up in this joyful confusion called life. It is presumptuous of me to say so, but I sense—and I say this in all humility—that you are a good man. I hope that you will not deny me the right to affirm our brotherhood, for in that brotherhood with all people I find the only basis for living. You, sir, are a representative of this government, and often unwillingly I too am a representative. With a profound feeling of inadequacy and unreadiness, I am forced by my conscience to stand as a representative of the suffering millions of Vietnam. I am forced to stand for the girl-child burned to death in Bin Hoa, for the refugee cold and hungry in a camp on the outskirts of Saigon, for the weary guerrilla fighter, for the Buddhist monk who is now a handful of ashes, for the thousands with no legs, thousands more with no eyes. Yes, Your Honor, I am representative even for the U.S. Marine now slowly dying in a Philadelphia hospital. These people, sir, are my constituency. I stand for them; and my word from them to this government, to this country, to both countries, is this: stop your war; your dominoes, your escalation, your computer theories. Your phony negotiations are at best human madness and at worst insidious, deliberate lies. Your war—all wars—are immoral and insane. Stop it.

"So here is Tom Rodd. I have tried, sir. Lord knows I have tried to obey this probation. I wanted to go to Selma and walk to Montgomery, but I didn't; I wanted to go to Washington and confront the President, but I didn't. I wanted to picket Girard College in Philadelphia, I wanted to help picket a nonunion store on Lancaster Avenue in West Philadelphia, but I didn't. But this war is too immediate, too pressing, too terrible, for me to say later, 'but I didn't.' What about the prison term I face? It's real, Your Honor; it scares me. But while I face isolation, my constituency faces death. My risk is minuscule compared to their reality. So, if prison comes, I will accept it and make the most of it. Now, let me reiterate what anybody who knows me should know: that I am an incorrigible optimist, that I love life. I play the banjo and daily toss my head and tap my feet to the romping stomping all-pervading beat of human existence. That's all I wanted to say, Your Honor, and I wish you and everybody a happy New Year."

III

The God Movement

*"You can't have great ideas in the
abstract. They have to take flesh. Jesus
had to have back of him a body
of people who would share his ideals,
share his convictions. . . .
The Christian movement resorted
more to fact than to argument.
Those people were the
direct evidence of 'the kingdom.'"*

THE DEMONSTRATION PLOT

The Semon on the Mount is really not a sermon at all—it is a lesson. It was an assignment which Jesus may have required his students to memorize. Its purpose was not to evoke inspiration but perspiration. It is obviously the gospel in working clothes. Jesus sets forth the core of the Christian faith, the manifesto of the Kingdom of God, or the God Movement. This is the body of thought, the guiding principles, which form, shape, correct, and direct the new order of the faithful and believing. It gives them substance, character, identity. In fact, Jesus felt that the whole Christian movement stands or falls on its response to this dazzling lecture (Matt. 7:24-27). Jesus was seeking to infuse his following with some ideas. The Jews considered themselves a theocracy through which God spoke to the people. So Jesus had to be a representative of God, giving God's platform to God's people.

We need to see that while Jesus presented this as his "platform" for his movement, there were certain things that he had to reject, certain ideas which could not be a part of his movement. Jesus had certain ideas thrown at him and he had to examine these ideas and weed them out, discard the bad ones and hold on to the good ones. In order to see the struggle he went through to get rid of the bad ideas, let's look in the fourth chapter of Matthew, verse one. Just prior to this, Jesus had come to John, who had recognized him as the Messiah, the anointed one of God, and had baptized him. Jesus is now ready to begin his public ministry. But before he can begin it he has to make it crystal clear to the people that certain ideas will *not* be a part of his movement.

And then Jesus was brought up into the wilderness by the Spirit to be tested out by the Confuser.

Now the word translated "devil" is *diabolos* in the Greek. It comes from *dia* meaning "around through," and *bollo* meaning "to throw." Our English word *ball* comes from that. *Diabolos* means "one who throws things about," one who stirs up things—gets them confused. The work of the devil is to just get us muddled. The Evil One never really takes a strong stand. He will raise the question. The old snake in the garden said to Eve, "Has God said not to eat of that tree?" He didn't say, "Don't you eat of it," or "Go ahead and eat of it." He just raised the question, in a good old discussion form. The work of the Confuser is to get Jesus out there and muddy the waters for him where he can't really see clearly any of these issues.

This is the form of a story. It doesn't have to be a historical fact. The Hebrew people always clothed great ideas in the language of drama and they never intended for people to get the stage props too seriously involved in the story. If you think Jesus was out there in the wilderness somewhere, and an old red devil with a pitchfork and a forked tail and horns came up, you haven't got it straight. This was all a back prop for this story.

When he had fasted forty days and forty nights, then he was hungry and the Confuser came to him and said, "If you are God's Son, tell these rocks that they should became loaves of bread."

"If you are God's son." This is not a theological question here. It has nothing to do with the deity or divinity of Jesus. This is a political question. Jesus was living under what the Jews called a theocracy—rule by God. So God has a son, or a deputy, or a vicar, on earth through whom he rules. This is actually about the same thing as saying, "If you want to be President of the United States. . . ." It has nothing to do with deity. It has something to do with his right to rule. If you are going to rule—to be the leader of this movement, tell these stones to become bread. Now, what's the proposition here? To get him a little loaf of bread and break his fast with it? No, this was not an appeal to Jesus' fleshly appetite. He had been fasting for forty days and forty nights. You don't break a fast with bread when you've been fasting that long.

The Confuser was saying, "Now Jesus, you want the people. You want to be head of this big movement. People are hungry. There's widespread unemployment. Everywhere people are crying for bread, bread, bread. Now, if you want to be at the head of your movement, make it a bread movement. Make bread as plentiful in Palestine as the stones are." The most plentiful thing in Palestine is stones. Somebody said that when God made the earth, he looked it over, thought it was lacking in something, and decided it needed a few rocks sprinkled over it. So he told two angels to go get a sack of rocks apiece and sprinkle them over the earth. One angel went out and sprinkled his around. The other angel started out and got right over Palestine and his sack busted. That's why whenever the Jews wanted to have a public execution, they stoned the victim— they wouldn't lack for ammunition anywhere, any time.

So this is a temptation to a movement of materialism—of atheistic materialism, such as we have in Moscow and Wall Street. Let life consist of the abundance of the things that people possess. Give everybody a Deepfreeze, give everybody wall-to-wall carpeting, give everybody a TV and two automobiles. Let prosperity run down like waters and economic abundance roll down like the mighty ocean. "If you can do that, Jesus, we think you can get the nomination."

Jesus rejected it and said, "No, I shall not have a movement of materialism, for man shall live not by bread alone, but by every word proceeding out of the mouth of God."

Man is not just a belly in search of bread. He's a soul in search of God. This is where the Communist philosophy has in it the seeds of its own destruction. It does not have an adequate concept of the nature of man. It conceives of man as a pure animal, who can be satisfied by the gratification of his fleshly appetites. Jesus admitted that men had to have bread, but they could not be satisfied with just bread.

Then the Confuser takes him into the holy city. And he sets him on the pinnacle of the temple and says, "If you are God's son, if you really want to be head of this God Movement, throw yourself down; for it has been written, 'He shall speak to his angels about you, and they shall carry you along on their hands, lest perhaps you stump your toe on a rock.'"

Here the pendulum swings to the opposite extreme. First is the proposition of pure, plain, blatant materialism. Jesus clearly rejects it. Now the pendulum swings all the way to the other extreme. And, in a figure of speech, Jesus is taken into the Holy City. Now, the Holy City was in the Holy Land, you remember. And it was located on the Holy Hill. And the Confuser takes him into the Holy Temple, which is in the middle of the Holy City. And he takes him up on the steeple of the temple. Now, you can't get any holier than that. You're at the top of holiness. You're at the jumping-off place. And that's exactly what Satan says to him.

"Now, Jesus I . . . I know it's true, you might not want this materialism stuff, but I . . . I see you're rather spiritual-minded. Let's set you up a big spiritual order. You can be the head of this vast ecclesiastical empire. You will be the executive secretary of the executive committee of the Southern Baptist Convention. If you don't want to be Stalin, maybe you want to be Pope. I got just the thing for you. You'll be at the head of this whole movement. It doesn't matter whether you jump off with some fuzzy theology or not, you'll have the cardinals under you—they'll catch you. And if they can't catch you the monsignors will. They'll never let you fall. You can issue any kind of papal bull, and it'll go through. You'll be un-fall-able, or infallible, as it may be. Don't have a movement of materialism, have a movement of ecclesiasticism. Be the head of a great church movement!"

Jesus rejects it. "Don't try out the Lord God with this organizational business. God didn't come to set up an ecclesiastical structure."

Well, this has really got Satan in a dilemma now. He doesn't know where to go. He's gone all the way from pure materialism to pure ecclesiasticism. And finally he says, "I got the thing you want. This is a hybrid. You know, the truth is always somewhere between the two extremes." So he takes him again up to a high mountain and he points out all the kingdoms of the world in their glory, and he says to him, "I'll give you all these things if you'll just fall down and worship me, Jesus. I'm really a kingmaker. I can make you king over all these political empires, if you'll just let me pull the strings." This is the temptation to political power based upon militarism. This was a temptation to become emperor—not pope, but emperor. "Here, you're a fine young fellow. You're not much older than Alexander the Great and he was a great emperor. You're just a bit younger than Julius Caesar. With your great social concern for people, you would make a much better emperor than Alexander or his father Philip, or Caesar, or any of these great men."

Jesus says, "Get going, Satan, for it has been written, 'You shall worship (that is, you shall give supreme loyalty) to the Lord, your God, and him alone shall you worship.' "

So Jesus rejected the three mightiest ideas that had bid for the mind of man—materialism, ecclesiasticism, and militarism. These three absolutely could not have any part in his movement. Having tested these big ideas, he turns to getting up his own platform on which to base his own movement.

Now, before he could do that, he had to have a following. He had to have people who would lend themselves to this idea. You cannot have great ideas in the abstract. They have to take flesh. They have to take form. Jesus had to have back of him a body of people, however large or small, who would share his ideals, share his convictions, and lend themselves to his movement. So immediately after rejecting these ideas which could not be a part of his movement, he turns himself to finding a body of people who would lend themselves to the new ideas which he would present to them.

From then on, Jesus began to cry out and to say, "Metanoeite, ēngiken gar hē basileia tōn ouranōn." (Change your whole way of thinking, for the new order of God's Spirit is confronting you.)

They translate that "Repent for the kingdom of heaven is at hand." But in the Greek it's much deeper than that. Much more vital than that. Change your whole way of thinking, for you are now confronted with the new order of God's Spirit. A whole new way of thinking is upon you. Change your old ideas, and get in with this new movement that's coming upon you.

Then walking beside the Sea of Galilee he saw Simon, who was called Petra.

Petra or *Petras* in the Greek means "Rock." Simon who was called Rock. His last name was Bar-Jonah or Son of John, or John's Son, or as we would say, "Johnson." So this is Rock Johnson and his brother.

Rock and Andy Johnson, his brother, threw their nets into the sea, for they were fishermen and he said to them, "Y'all come with me and I'll make you to be fishers of men."

Now, they might have gotten to talking about the holy vocation of fishing for fish. And Rock might have said, "Well, you know, we'd like to go with you and all that, but can't a deacon be a good fisher of fish? Do you want me to give up my nets and boats and all? I just got started in this thing. Andy and I just bought our new boat. Nice fiber-glass job."

I can see the name on the boat: "Johnson Brothers." These are young men who are ambitious. And no doubt they had just come from a conference that had talked about the holiness of all vocations—how you can be a Christian just as well fishing for fish as for men. But Jesus said, "I've got to have you, boys. Come on." And they went. You know, it just could be that there are times when Jesus calls on us to get out of what we're doing! God said to Abraham, "Get out of this country that you're living in, into a land that I'll show you." Could be that there are a lot of Christians that ought to change their vocations.

Then he went a little farther and he found James (down our way we call him Jim) *Zebedee and John, his brother* (most folks down there named John, they call Jack)—*Jim and Jack Zebedee in the boat with their father mending their nets.*

Their old nets were about shot. This wasn't "Johnson Brothers," this was "Zebedee & Son." This was an old-line business, founded in 1862. The old man and his boys had been in business a long time. And Jesus called them. Now they might have said, "You know, pap's been in this business a long time—it's an old family business. We built up a special trade with a particular type of gourmet sardine. We just don't want to break up this old business. Now we'll give you a tenth. We'll tithe. But we're going to stay in old Grandpa Zebedee's business." But these boys had to get out into a business that Jesus could put them in.

Now, we don't get this in this little episode here, but when you read the list of these twelve, you find some interesting characters in it. It's pretty heavy with fishermen, but fishing was the major occupation of that day. Other occupations and other ideologies are reflected in the list. Jesus chose Matthew. Now, that's an unfortunate choice for a man who's trying to get a popular movement going. He was one of the most unpopular men of Jesus' day. He was a publican, a tax gatherer for the Romans. Publicans almost without exception were Jews—renegade Jews collecting taxes for the hated Roman government.

And then to top it off, Jesus chose a guy by the name of Simon the Zealot. We know the creed of the zealots: no king but Jehovah (they wouldn't recognize the Roman emperor), no lawgiver but Moses (they wouldn't accept the decisions of the Federal Supreme Court over in Rome), and no tax but the temple tax. Can you imagine patriotism on a higher plane than that? All you would have to do is strike up one strain of "Dixie" and those boys would be out there waving the Confederate flag. One of the things you had to do when you became a zealot was to take an oath that if opportunity ever afforded itself you would assassinate publicans.

Now, Jesus chose Matthew the Publican and Simon the Zealot. I'll bet you one thing—on more than one night Jesus had to sleep between those two boys. The only thing that kept Simon's knife out of Matthew's ribs was Jesus. But if Jesus could make Simon the Zealot and Matthew the Publican walk down the main street in Jerusalem, holding hands and calling one another "Brother," the God Movement was here! This was to be a demonstration plot —not so much a preaching platform, but a demonstration plot that the God Movement was under way.

Jesus was trying to make a concrete, living demonstration of the God Movement. When we read that Jesus said to the Pharisees, "The Kingdom of God is within you," he did not use the word *within*. The kingdom of God was not "within" the Pharisees. The word did not mean "inside of you"—it meant "in your midst." He was not talking about the Kingdom of God in an abstract sense. He was saying, "The Kingdom of God is in your midst." Where? "Right here. Here they are. Here are the fellows. This is the God Movement—right in your midst—and you are being confronted with it." The Christian movement resorted more to fact than to argument. Those people were the direct evidence of the "kingdom"—the God Movement.

THE LESSON ON THE MOUNT—I

When he saw the multitudes he went up on the hill, and when he had sat down his students came to him, and he opened his mouth and taught them.

Bear in mind that he taught them. This is not a sermon. This is the *Lesson* on the Mount. There's a difference between a sermon and a lesson. A sermon is something you sleep through and tell the preacher you enjoyed. But a lesson is something which is assigned and for which you are held responsible. You don't sleep through lessons, only sermons.

Some people have said that it is a collection of Jesus' sayings. I don't think it's a collection. I think he put them together in a whole, and that this was his platform. I believe every one of his twelve disciples could have repeated it verbatim. You could have awakened old Peter at three o'clock in the morning, "Peter, Peter, the house is on fire." He would have sat straight up in bed and said, "Blessed are the poor in spirit, for theirs is the kingdom of God. Blessed are they that mourn. . . ." He would've known that thing through and through. I think that any one of the twelve would have known it. All Jesus would've had to say is, "Andy, start on Matthew 5:18." Andy could have picked it right up. "How about it, Jim; you got that?" "Yessir." "Gimme Matthew 6:1." He would have started right on with it. Those fellows had been drilled in it, for this was the doctrine, these were the very ideas that were to shape their existence. I think the memorization of the Lesson on the Mount should be at least one requirement for membership in a church.

Jesus begins the lesson by taking us up the stair steps, so to speak, into this new order. These so-called Beatitudes are not so much separated verses, as I was taught in Sunday school. These are great ideas governing the development of the Movement. They are stair steps into this new order. They are stages of the metamorphosis, the process of changing one's whole philosophy of life. He begins on the very lowest step: *Blessed are the poor in spirit...*

I have tried everywhere to find an English word that would actually translate this Greek word *makarios*. Some translate it "happy." Some translate it "fortunate." Some translate it "blessed." All those elements are in this word, but they still do not fully contain it. It really means to be in a relationship—not a state of joy or happiness, but in a relationship. It means to have the deep security that comes from loving and being loved. It means to have the deep soul-satisfying experience of being in a fellowship of which you feel that you are a part and you're carried along with it. To be in union with God and with the other brothers on the team. It's the joy of being on a team that's playing and going somewhere. It isn't just fortunate or happy or blessed. It's deeper, much deeper than that. I just don't know an English word that will translate it. I translated it, "to be God's people"— that is, to be in a fellowship of brethren who both love one another and love God. That is the joy, that is the blessing, that's talked about here. So I'm going to translate it this way: *"The spiritually humble are God's people, for they are citizens of his new order."*

Now, to be poor in spirit means to recognize yourself as a spiritual pauper, that within yourself, and even within the fellowship of which you are a part, there is no real abiding strength or power; to recognize there is any strength, it must come from above. This must be God's movement. It cannot he a human type of thing. It can't be a religious Kiwanis Club or Rotary Club. It has to be the work of God's doing. Only those who recognize that can ever be a part of God's new order. He is its power. He is its strength. He is its wisdom. He is its morning and its night. God alone infuses it and empowers it. As Paul puts it, "Our little *koinonia,* our little fellowship is not a human organization, but it is created by God himself."

Secondly, Jesus says, *"They who are concerned to the point of action shall see their concerns fulfilled."*

This doesn't mean to just weep, to go along with tears in your eyes and a long face. God knows we have had enough of that. *Mourn* here means to be so deeply concerned that you're willing to get up and do something about it no matter what the cost may be to you. We might translate it thus, "They who act on their convictions are God's people, for they will see their ideas become reality."

They who wear God's bridle are his people, and they will be his partners across the land.

Usually this is "Blessed are the meek." This word *meek* in the Greek is used only two other times in the Bible to describe people. It's used to describe one Old Testament character, Moses, and one New Testament character, Jesus. We have translated this word to mean a Mr. Milquetoast type of character, just giving in, being all things to all people, a kind of a spiritual door mat for humanity. But can you imagine Moses walking in, saying, "Good morning, Mr. Pharaoh. How are you this morning? Would you mind, please sir, letting my people go out on a little two-hour picnic?" No! *That* isn't meekness! Moses walked in there and said, "Thus sayeth the Lord. Let my people go!" That's being meek.

What does this word *meek* mean, anyway? It's used almost entirely in the classic Greek to refer to horses. Coming from a farm in south Georgia, I know what this word means because down there, while we don't have many horses, we have mules. And I think this word means not a meek mule, but a broke mule. I bought a mule one time. The fellow told me he wasn't broke, but he'd knock off $25 if I would break him. Later I would have given him $100 to take his old mule back!

"Blessed are the broke." I don't mean the flat broke now, but those who have been trained to wear the bridle. When the Sanhedrin told Peter and John, "Don't you ever preach in the name of this Jesus any more—we just got rid of the guy," Peter said to that austere body, "Whether it be right for us to obey God or man, you judge. But we cannot but speak those things which we have seen and heard." That's one of the meekest statements in the Bible. The "meek" man is the man who obeys the pull of God, who never tunes his ears to the whispering of society, who isn't afraid to lose his influence or his head, who's got no better sense than to be a fool for God! That's the meek. They aren't weak, insipid, inane little two-by-four Christians who never stir up anybody. These meek folks are the folks who turn the world upside down. And God said, "They'll be my partners across the land."

They who have an unsatisfied appetite for the right are God's people and they will be given plenty to chew on. The generous are God's people, and they will be treated generously. They whose motives are pure are God's people, and they will have spiritual insight.

The word *pure-in-heart* there is the Greek word *katharos*. It means "to be scoured." So Jesus is saying, those whose motives are unadulterated will gain insight. Their eye is single. They're not trying to look at money on this side and popularity over there. These are the people whose eyes are in focus on the one object. Their motives are pure or we might say "single." To them the issue is not muddied up by Satan. Jesus was truly pure in heart when he kept his eyes solely on God and didn't allow Satan to muddy the waters by injecting all these other issues into his platform.

You all are the earth's salt. But now if you just sit there and don't salt, how will the world ever get salted? You'll be so worthless that you will be thrown out and trampled on by the rest of society. You all are the world's light; you are a city on a hill that cannot be hid. Have you ever heard of anybody turning on a light and then covering it up? Don't you fix it so that it will light up the whole room? Well, then, since you are God's light which he has turned on, go ahead and shine so clearly that when your conduct is observed it will plainly be the work of your spiritual Father.

This is something which it seems to me the Christian fellowship really needs to get through its thick hide. I don't know of anything that has caused me more real suffering and real anxiety than to see the Christian Church sit in this great social revolution which is rocking the Southland, and our whole nation, as though nothing were transpiring, keeping God's salt in a saltcellar that we call the sanctuary. The Lord is in his holy temple; let all the earth keep silence before him . . . especially silence! I had a preacher friend tell me not too long ago, "Clarence, we've just got to lay low on this thing, and let it all blow over, and when it all blows over, then you can afford to take a stand on it." I said, "Reverend, do you feel that way about sin in general? Are you going to wait until sin just blows over? Then you're going to hop up and say, 'I'm agin' it!' Glory be."

Jesus said to the religious people of his day, "You-all are like graves which appear not and men walk over unawares." He said, "You religious folks [talking to the Pharisees] are like unmarked graves of which there is no longer any evidence and men walk over you without being aware that there's even a corpse there. There was a time when at least you had the capacity to raise a stink, but you've even lost that. And you make about as much impact on the world as a corpse that's been dead and buried so long that there's not even any fresh dirt left." I sometimes wonder if that isn't about how effective we Christians are in this society of ours. The work of the salt is to salt. And the work of the light is to shine, not to hide itself until the darkness disappears.

Don't you all ever think for one moment that I'm trying to destroy the moral and religious principles of our [Southern] way of life. My purpose is not to destroy them, but to establish them, for I tell you truthfully that so long as heaven and earth remain, not one dotting of an "I" or crossing of a "T" will be eliminated from our highest and noblest ideals until every one of them becomes a reality. So then, if anyone disregards one of the least of

Men of peace and good will are God's people, and will be known as his children. They who have endured much for what's right are God's people. They are citizens of his new order.

They who have endured much for what's right are God's people. It does not say: You all are God's people when you increase your budget 20 per cent every year; you all are God's people when you have the best choir in the city; you all are God's people when you get your sanctuary air-conditioned.

You all are God's people when others call you names and harass you and tell all kinds of false tales on you just because you follow me. Be cheerful and good-humored, because your spiritual advantage is great, for that's the way they treated men of conscience in the past.

If somebody hasn't called you up at two o'clock in the morning and threatened to kill you the next time they see you, what's the matter with you? Where have you been? They're going to call you, he says, all kinds of names. I know what they're going to call you. They're going to call you "Communist!" Any Christian who hasn't been called a Communist today, I don't think he's worth his salt.

"Be cheerful and good-humored." Now, I haven't reached that stage of maturity yet. When that phone rings at two o'clock in the morning and some vile-mouth guy starts calling me names and threatens to kill me, I tell you I just ain't cheerful. I don't think Jesus really means that you've got to pretend to cheerfulness. I think what he's saying is, "Don't let those guys get you down." My good friend Patty Boyle, author of *The Desegregated Heart,* has had wooden crosses burned on her lawn. She's got a little motto hanging in her hall right over an old oil-soaked cross that was burned on her lawn, and which she doused and brought into her hallway. She's got a little sign hanging over it with a quotation from Vinegar Joe Stilwell. It says, "Carborundum non illigitimus," which freely translated means, "Don't let the s.o.b.'s get you down."

I think what Jesus is saying here is, "Don't let them get you down, boy." Keep a good attitude. Keep your sense of humor. If you don't learn to laugh at the devil, he'll whip you sure as everything. You've got to stay in a good humor. It's the only way you can survive it. "Be good-humored," Jesus said, "knowing that you got just what all the others got. Don't ask for any special consideration. This is just the world's way of letting you know that you're in a long line of succession of those who have loved God and sought to follow him."

*these God-given principles, and encourages others to do so, he
shall be considered unimportant in God's new order of the Spirit.
But whoever lives by them and upholds them shall be considered
vital to the spiritual movement.*

*Let me tell you-all something else, unless your conduct is better
than that of usual, ordinary, religious people, you'll never make
the grade into God's new order of the Spirit. For example, you've
always been told, "Don't murder," and "If anybody does murder,
he shall be brought to judgment." But I'm telling you that everyone who nurses a grudge against his fellow man shall be brought
into judgment. And anyone who spits in the face of his brother
man stands condemned, and whoever yells, "You lowdown so-
and-so!" shall be roasted in hell's fires. So then, if you are in worship services and keep remembering all the things your brother
has against you, leave the sanctuary and go look up the one you
have wronged and straighten things out with him. Only then may
you return to church.*

*Be courteous at all times toward an opponent. Otherwise, you
might be dragged into court, turned over to the sheriff and thrown
into the clink. I'm telling you a fact, you won't get out of there
until you pay the last cent of your fine.*

He's saying, "The old law, the old tradition, said 'Don't murder.' But I want to really explain to you what murder is. Murder
has its beginnings in the heart of man—way back in his attitudes,
in his motives. Anyone who has contempt for his fellow man, who
looks upon him as a nobody, as inferior, there murder actually
begins." In Jesus' day one of the worst things you could do to a
man was to spit in his face—it still isn't too polite—and Jesus is
saying that murder begins at the point where you spit on a man
with contempt. Whenever you call him a lowdown so-and-so—a
nigger, a wop, a Chink—it's at that point, in the attitude, that you
become a murderer. He's transferring the law from an external,
legal frame to the deep inner workings of the heart. His people
will be people of the spirit—not people of legal, external frame-
work.

He takes up the law about adultery:

*You've heard it said, don't sleep with someone you're not mar-
ried to. But I want to tell you, whoever sets his eye on a woman
with hope of intercourse with her, has already slept with her in
his mind. So if your right eye becomes hopelessly infected, have it
cut out and thrown away, because it is better to lose one of your
organs than to lose your body. Or if your right hand becomes hope-*

*lessly infected, cut it off and throw it away, because it is better to
lose one of your limbs than to lose your whole body.*

Now what he's saying here is simply that sex, like a hand or an
eye, is a God-given thing. There's no evil in it. It is given by God
for a good purpose, just as the eye is given for a good purpose and
the hand is given for a good purpose. But there is such a thing as
a good thing's becoming perverted and becoming the focal point
of infection. Just as the eye may get infected and cause the destruction of the whole body, or just as the hand may become infected
and cause the destruction of the whole body, so it is that a perverted use of sex may cause the destruction of the whole person-
ality. Jesus would say that it would be much better to forgo sex
entirely than to let it be the means of blighting the whole person-
ality and damning the soul.

Jesus is saying here, "This adultery I'm talking about goes way
back into the inner motives. The fact that lack of opportunity or
circumstance may hold a man in check does not change the inner,
adulterous nature of the heart." It's somewhat as though a man has
a very vicious dog, and he chains that dog to a strong post with a
heavy chain. And he always says to his neighbor, "Why, my dog
has never bitten anybody." That might be true, but that dog's
goodness is in direct proportion to the strength of the chain and
the size of the post. Remove the chain and remove the post and
you'll see the real nature of that dog. Now Jesus is saying the mere
fact that a man is chained by law or circumstance does not change
the inner nature of the man.

*It has also been said, if a man divorces his wife let him give her
a certificate that she is free. But I'm telling you-all, anybody who
divorces his wife, except for sleeping with another man, causes
her to have had unlawful intercourse, and whoever marries one
so divorced also has unlawful intercourse.*

*Again you've heard it said by the old folks, "Don't break your
oath, and always keep a solemn oath to the Lord." But I'm telling
you not to make any oaths at all—not by the heaven as God's
throne, or by the earth as his footrest, or by Atlanta as "the city
of the governor." Don't make any oath even by your head, because
you can't make one hair white or black. Instead, let your word be
a straightforward Yes or No.*

This is not talking about profanity. In those days the Jews had
a banking system, and they had a way of putting up collateral.
You could go into a banker and say, "Mr. Banker, I want to borrow $100." "O.K. You got any collateral?" "Yes, sir, I want to put

up my hand. I want to pledge by my hand." "Well, all right. Could you give me a little more than that?" "Well, I could give you my neck." If you put up that much you're going to be there to pay that note. In other words, the pledge depended on what you swore by. If you wanted to borrow a big sum of money you would pledge by the Holy City. And if you really got a big loan you would pledge by "the earth as God's footstool."

I remember an old farmer went to my daddy (he used to be a banker) and wanted to put up his old mule and get some money. Daddy says, "All right, describe the mule." He said, "Well, Mr. Jim, he's 23 years old. He's blind in one eye and ain't got no teeth, and he's crippled." Daddy said, "What in the world do you keep a mule like that for?" He said, "For collateral."

You see, putting up collateral is nothing but adding to your promise and guaranteeing it by something that you possess.

THE LESSON ON THE MOUNT—II

You've also heard the saying, "Take an eye for an eye; take a tooth for a tooth." But I'm telling you, never respond with evil.

In some translations that is translated "do not resist him who is evil" or "do not resist evil." The Greek has three cases, all with the same case ending—the locative, the instrumental, and the dative. The context of the word has to tell you which case it is in. Now, if this word is in the dative case, it should be translated: "Do not resist a person who is evil." But I really can't imagine our Lord saying that, for he surely did resist evil people. He preached with all his heart against them. It could be locative, in which case it should be translated: "Do not resist when you find yourself in the presence of evil." Certainly that does not fit with the context. Or it could be instrumental—that is: "Do not resist with evil." Do not use evil as the instrument of your resistance. If someone slaps you, you don't slap him back.

Instead, if somebody slaps you on your right cheek, offer him the other one too. And if anybody wants to drag you into court and take away your shirt, let him have your undershirt. If somebody makes you go a mile for him, go two miles. Give to him who asks of you, and don't turn your back on anyone who wants a loan.

Another thing you've always heard is, "Love your own group and hate the hostile outsider." But I'm telling you, love the outsiders and pray for those who try to do you in, so that you might

*be sons of your spiritual Father. For he lets his sun rise on both
sinners and saints, and he sends rain on both good people and
bad. Listen here, if you love only those who love you, what is your
advantage? Don't even scalawags do that much? And if you speak
to no one but your friends, how are you any different? Do not the
non-Christians do as much? Now you, you-all must be mature, as
your spiritual Father is mature.*

Beyond all doubt, man's most vexing problem, from prehistoric
times to the present, has been learning how to respond maturely
to those who oppose him. We have learned how to respond to our
friends, but to respond to our enemies—that is the problem. How
can we be mature? How can we make a grownup response to people who want to do us in, to hound us, to beat us, to persecute us?
We would expect our Lord to be quite clear in his teachings on
this subject, and he is. He begins by going deep back into history
and digging up various responses that men have made, and I
think all of us will respond in one of the four ways with which
our Lord dealt.

One is the method of unlimited retaliation. Somebody knocks
out your eye, you knock both of his out. Somebody knocks out
your tooth, you knock all his out if you can get to him. If somebody kills your dog, you kill his cow. If he kills your cow, you kill
his mule. If he kills your mule, you kill him! No limit to the
amount of retaliation. Unbridled anger. Unbridled vengeance.
Now, mankind seems early to have outgrown this idea, but has
lapsed back into it with the invention of the atom bomb. This
seems to be the principle which dominates the State Departments
of most so-called civilized nations. You bomb us, we'll obliterate
you. You bomb a little city, we will annihilate a whole nation.
Unlimited, massive retaliation.

Now this is so childish, so barbaric, so beastly that it never occurred to our Lord that anyone within his hearing would ever
resort to it. He picked it up there, and said,

"But now wait. If somebody knocks out your eye, don't knock
both his eyes out. Moses said, 'One eye for an eye. One tooth for a
tooth.' If he knocks out your eye, don't knock them both out, just
knock out one eye. If he knocks out your tooth, don't knock out all
of his teeth, just knock out one tooth." This was the first effort at
restraint on the strong. Now, he says, "Moses gave you that idea,
but it is not enough. Let us move on up to another one." The old
prophets came along and said, "Love your neighbor, and hate your
enemy." This was the first glimmerings of limited love. If your

neighbor knocks out your tooth, forgive him. But if he's a person of another race or another nation, give him the works. In other words, limit your love to your own little group, your own nation, your own race. This is the rule of limited love. This concept enables men to live together as nations, limiting their love to their own nation, but it does not enable them to live together as a world family.

This seems to be the place that most of us really are at today. We love America, and limit our love to the shores and the boundaries of the United States. I think most of us reflect the idea that's inscribed on an old tombstone down in Mississippi. It says, "Here lies J.H.S. In his lifetime, he killed 99 Indians, and lived in the blessed hope of making it 100, until he fell asleep in the arms of Jesus." Now, Indians don't count. Ninety-nine of them, and you can live in "the blessed hope" of getting just one more to round it out at an even hundred and still fall asleep in the arms of Jesus. But if you had killed just one white man, you'd fall asleep in a noose. You see, it's all right to kill Indians because we don't care about Indians, but you better not kill a white man. So, a nation can drop an atom bomb on brown people, yellow people, and annihilate two whole cities of people and we give him the Congressional medal. If he kills one man in the United States, we give him the electric chair.

That's loving your neighbor, those of your own race, your own group. Down in Georgia, an integrated group of kids working in the civil rights movement ran out of gas while they were out in the country. Two of the white ones decided they'd go for gas. So they came to a farmer and asked him if he had gas. "Yes, sure," he said, and he got them a gallon of gas and said, "Where's your car?" They said, "About a mile up the road." And he said, "Well, get in. I'll take you up there," and they said, "No, we'll walk." And he said, "Why, no, it's too hot. I wouldn't think about letting you walk! Get in!" "No," they said, "Uh, we . . . we'd just rather walk. We need the exercise." He said, "No, it's too hot. Come on. Get in. I'll take you up there." So very reluctantly, the two white kids got in with this white farmer and they drove along to the car. They stopped and got out and the farmer realized it was some of those integrationists. He became infuriated! He grabbed the can, put it back in his car, and drove off in a huff. If they had been all-white, he would have been a fine Southern gentleman, a deacon in the Baptist church, asleep in the arms of Jesus. But now he was dealing with people of a different race and he can't love *those* people.

Jesus said it is not enough to limit your love to your own nation, to your own race, to your own group. You must respond with love even to those outside of it, respond with love to those who hate you. This concept enables men to live together not as nations, but as the human race. We are now at the stage of history where we will either take this step or perish. For we have learned with consummate skill to destroy mankind. We have learned how to efficiently annihilate the human race. But, somehow or other, we shrink with horror from the prospect not of annihilation, but of reconciliation. We will either be reconciled—we shall love one another—or we shall perish.

Now, Jesus did not advocate nonviolence. He was not advocating passive resistance. He does not say, "If your enemy slaps you on your right cheek, put on a demonstration protesting your rights." He is not commanding us to demand our rights. The only right love has is the right to give itself. Now this at times may be passive. That is, you may do nothing to a man who opposes you. I was at the Sumter County livestock sale some time back buying calves and was just about to leave when the town's archsegregationist came in. Well, I didn't want to have a consultation with him at that moment, so I kind of shrunk down behind everybody else and looked for a mousehole but couldn't find one, and finally he came in and looked all around and saw me. He came over and stood about two or three feet in front of me and yelled at the top of his voice—even above the noise of the auctioneer—"Here's that old Jordan fellow, folks! We ain't killed him yet, but we can kill him now. We got him here by hisself!" Well, I started looking for even a knothole to get through at that time, but I couldn't find one. And then he looked at me and raised his voice again. He said, "You ain't nothin' but a ——" Well, he made a positive statement that on my mother's side, I had some canine ancestry. Now, down where I come from, when somebody attributes to you that kind of pedigree, you're supposed to respond. And I felt my fist getting into position to respond. And then, about that time, he used God's name and called me that kind of a —— Named me that kind of a pedigree. Then he took a little deeper breath and called me something else and I noticed that, while he didn't have any teeth, he did have tonsils, and I thought that this would be a nice time to perform a public tonsillectomy. But somehow God gave me the power to restrain myself while the little fellow kept on calling me increasingly long names. I didn't know there were that many species around until he called me those names.

Well, he finally gave up and went outside. Now, there was a big old 200-pound farmer sitting next to me and I noticed every time this fellow would call me by one of those names, this farmer would kind of wince. Finally, this farmer moved over next to me and said, "You know what?" I thought he was getting ready to take up where this little fellow had just left off. I said, *"What?"* He said, "I want to know how come you didn't hit that little fellow? You could have beat the —— You could have really whopped him with one arm tied behind your back." I said, "I think that is a correct appraisal of the situation." He said, "Well, how come you didn't hit him?" I said, "My friend, there are two reasons why I didn't hit him. One's purely selfish. If I'd a hit that little segregationist, everybody in this sale barn would have jumped on me and mopped up the floor with me. And I just don't want my wife married to a mop. That's one reason I didn't hit him. But the real reason was I'm trying to be a follower of Jesus Christ and he has taught me to love my enemies. Now, while I must confess I had the minimum amount of love for this little fellow at the time, at least I did him no harm." And this old fellow said, "Is *that* what it means to be a Christian?" I said, "Friend, that isn't all that it means, but that's a part of it." We sat for a while talking about being a Christian.

So I might say that it is not enough to just merely not harm your enemies. Somehow or another, we must go beyond that. Love is not merely a weapon. It is not a strategy, and it may or may not work. To do good to those who hate you is such stupendous folly it can't be expected to work. Love didn't work for Jesus. No man has ever loved as he loved, but it didn't work. He wound up on a cross. And yet, it *does* work if your motive is *not* to make it work. Love works in the home. But if you say, "Well, you know, it really works to love your wife. If you love her, she'll darn your socks and bake you pie every day." If that is the motive for love, I doubt that your wife will darn your socks or bake pies. But love does work. I think Abraham Lincoln said it so well one day. Congressman Thaddeus Stevens, a bitter man from Massachusetts, shared the sentiment in the North to just crush the South after the war was over. When Mr. Lincoln was advocating binding up the wounds of the nation, and ideas such as forgiveness, reconciliation, Thaddeus Stevens pounded the table and said, "Mr. Lincoln! I think enemies ought to be *destroyed!*" Mr. Lincoln quietly said, "Mr. Stevens, do not I destroy my enemy when I make him my friend?"

In the long run, it is the only way that really does work. For when the cards are all in, and the final chapter of history is written, when time is rolled up as a garment, and God is all and in all —on that final day, it will be the peacemakers, not the warriors, who will be called the sons of God.

However, I don't think Jesus would point to love with this Dale Carnegie talk that you can win friends and influence people this way. I don't think he was bargaining, saying, "Well, if you love your enemy, you'll make a good man out of him, you'll convert him, he'll finally turn and be softhearted toward you." No. I don't think Jesus was that naive. I've been in a situation where I've tried to love my enemy and I haven't seen many of them converted. Jesus wasn't making that bargain to try to save our hides, to say, "Well, if you love your enemy, it's practical. It's the only practical thing to do." I don't think it's very practical to love a man who's trying to shoot you and kill you.

I've changed this a little bit in my application in the South. Jesus said, "If a man smites you on your right cheek, you turn to him the other one." Well, when he smites me on the right cheek, I turn to him both heels. I get out of there. I don't stay around to tell him how much I love him. In the long run, however, I think Jesus is saying, "I want you to love your enemies so that you may be sons of your Father." For this is his response to those who oppose him. He lets the sun shine on people irrespective of their attitude towards him, and he lets the rain fall on people irrespective of their attitude towards him.

He said, "I want you to be mature." This word is translated "perfect" ("Be ye therefore perfect as your heavenly Father is perfect"), but this is not a correct translation. The word means "perfect" in the sense of being whole, being all there, having all the parts, being "mature." "I want you to grow up. I want you to be mature in your reactions and in your responses just like the Father is mature in his reactions and responses. I don't want you to react like a little bunch of kindergarten folk smacking one another and beating one another over the head. I don't want you to be like a bunch of adolescents who have only control enough to limit themselves to the amount of evil that they give to each other. I don't want you to be a bunch of teen-agers who are limiting their love to their own little social clique. I want you to be a mature son of God. Grow up and be a full-grown Christian!"

I don't think Jesus has a right to expect perfection of any of us folks, but I do think he has the right to expect maturity. I think he does have a right to expect us to act like adults. Jesus said, I want you to have this unlimited love, not that you might convert your enemies or work up a bargain with them, not because it's practical, but because this is the mature response of your Father. This is the way He responds and, therefore, I want you to respond in that same way.

This has been a very difficult thing for Christians to understand. We always try to explain it away and say, "Yeah, but there are some people you can't love. If you love them, they'll just come over and take you over and kill you and destroy. There are some people you just can't love."

I don't think you're going to get to first base with Jesus on that kind of stuff. He knew there were people who couldn't be loved too, but he loved them right on. He knew there were people who would respond with sneers, who would respond with spit; they would respond with nails through his hands and spears through his side. He knew about these unlovable characters. I can imagine old Rock Johnson out there that night when those guys from the religious headquarters came to get his friend, thinking something like this: Now it's one thing to turn your cheek. But when you got loved ones and somebody's trying to get them you got no right to turn the cheek. Jesus is the best friend I have. I love him more than anyone I've ever known. I would die for him. So if anybody ever puts their cotton-picking finger on him, they're going to have *me* to deal with!

So out there that night old Rock had a sword on each side. And when those fellows came to grab Jesus, Rock pulled out his sword and started whopping. He was aiming at that guy's neck, but the guy ducked and the sword just clipped off his ear. He wanted to get his head. I think Peter was ready to swing again when Jesus said, "Rock, put that sword back! They that live by the sword shall die by the sword." And then he reached down and picked the guy's ear up, rubbed the sand off and put it back on. Don't tell me Jesus didn't know about enemies that were bad and unlovable. He knew them quite well. He knew what they'd do to you. He knew they'd come out and hang you on a cross if you loved 'em. But he still says you're going to have to love them.

I don't know how we reconcile this with our attitudes today. "Well, you love these Russians, they're going to come over here and kill you and take your country." I don't know. Maybe they will. The first Christians had it pretty rough and I don't know that he can promise anything better than that to us. There is such a thing, though, as keeping good will in a very difficult situation. Last fall, several of my friends were arrested in Americus. One of the young fellows was from Koinonia. He was a Jewish lad. He had been working at Koinonia helping us to organize a farmer's co-operative for Negro farmers. And he was walking down the street of Americus and the police laid their hands on him, along with three others, threw him in jail, and charged all four with insurrection.

There's an old law in Georgia that makes insurrection a capital offense. He was held in jail four or five months without bond because his offense was one that was punishable by death. During that time we tried to stay in communication with him by smuggling letters in and out through a trusty. On one occasion this young Jewish lad wrote a letter in which he intimated that his life was in great danger—not from the prison authorities, but from his cellmates. The sheriff constantly reminded these cellmates that this boy was what he called "a nigger lover."

Now I want to quote from this Jewish boy because it reminds me so much of another Jewish young fellow who said almost the same thing, many many years ago. This is a quotation from a letter that came forth on a little piece of crumpled brown wrapping paper that he had written and wadded up and passed to the trusty. The trusty passed it to someone else and it was finally delivered a few days later.

"Though there is now no immediate threat, there have been challenges to fight and the danger will probably recur. I won't hit back under any circumstances. I want so badly to live and to get out of here, but if I am killed, perhaps I can still dry some tears and bring some joy. If I die, please see to it that my eyes or any other organs or parts of my body that can be used for transplants or other medical uses are donated to those uses. Then, please bury what's left of my body as it is without any box or coffin or any of that stuff, or embalming or fancy clothes other than what happens to be on the body, and then bury it at Koinonia. Just please plant a tree, a plum or a fig or a peach or a pecan, something that bears sweet fruit and has a long life, so that it may use what remains of my body to make pleasures for the children of my brothers here in Sumter County. Please see to it that no revenge or punishment or prosecution is taken against those of my brothers who have struck me down, but only that Sumter County officials be enjoined from putting a man ever again, no matter of what heinous crime accused, in the exposed position I'm in here. Thank you so much. May you all be blessed."

He does not bear the name of Christ, but he surely bears the spirit of a noble Jew who had seen that one must love his enemies regardless of what that enemy does.

It seems to me that we Christians have an idea here that the world is tremendously in need of. When we're tottering fearfully on the brink of utter annihilation, looking so desperately for hope from somewhere, walking in deep darkness, looking for one little streak of light, do not we Christians have some light? Can't we say, "Sure, we know the way. It's the way of love and of peace. We shall not confront the world with guns in our hands and bombs behind our backs. We shall confront the world without fear, with utter helplessness except for the strength of God."

(EDITOR'S NOTE: The following remarks are lifted from a different discussion on a related subject.)

There are one or two passages which seem to imply that you should give unconditional loyalty to the emperor. One place is the thirteenth chapter of Romans, and I'm not at all sure that Paul, there, means you should give unconditional commitment to the emperor. At the end of the twelfth chapter of Romans, Paul says:

For it is written "vengeance is my job. I will tend to it, says the Lord." But if your enemy hungers, feed him; if he thirsts, water him, for by doing this you'll fill his little noggin with lighted charcoal. Now, don't you be overwhelmed by evil, but you overwhelm evil with good.

You see, he's making a good pacifist sermon here. And then all of a sudden he says, "Let every soul be in subjection to the powers that be." Now, how are we to reconcile this? Suppose the powers that be aren't in favor of overwhelming the enemy with good? Suppose they aren't in favor of giving him bread and water? Suppose they're in favor of taking vengeance into their own hands? What do you do? Well, actually, Paul is saying that "every soul"—including the Roman emperor, the President, the King—should be in subjection to the overarching powers, the powers that really are. In other words, he's saying, let the Emperor, let the bishop, let the Pope, let the preacher, let every soul be in subjection to God's overarching power. If he won't be in subjection to the overarching power, he's got no right to ask you to be in subjection to his power. If he is undisciplined to a higher power, how can he then ask you to be disciplined in respect to his power? You are not called upon to be in total abject obedience to every little Hitler that struts across the face of the earth. No Christian would swallow that and Paul wouldn't swallow it. If the authority will himself be in subjection, then you can be in subjection to him, for it is ordained of God provided he himself is in subjection to God. So the Christian is always having to draw this line, following the people over him so long as they follow God. When they refuse, then you've got to get out of line.

WAS JESUS REALLY POOR?

Reading from the fifth chapter of James, verse one:

And you rich guys, hold on a minute. You-all get ready to moan and groan because of the hardships that are coming on you. Your piles of gadgets are broken down. Your electric furnace won't work. The air conditioning's busted. And all your pretty clothes are full of holes. Your stocks and bonds are worthless. Inflation's hit you, and the certificates shall be evidence against you and will gnaw at your hearts like a flame. You pile them up for the judgment day.

Now listen. The wages of the workers who till your plantations and them you've cheated are crying out and the pitiful pleas of your laborers have been heard by the Lord of Redress.

He seems to be assuming here that any man who's wealthy stole it from somebody. You've got to get it from your laborers or from somewhere. You can't make that much.

You've gorged at the posh restaurants and whooped it up at the swank hotels, even at your national conventions. You'll fatten yourselves like a slaughterhouse steer and when you get that fat, you're ready to be killed, ready to be slaughtered. You arrest and kill even an innocent person who offers no resistance. But you, brothers of mine, hold on till the Lord's movement gets going. Look how the farmer awaits the precious harvest of his land, staying by it until it receives both spring and summer rains. You too hold on and pep up your hearts because the Lord's movement is right here.

Now, let's turn to the Sermon on the Mount, Matthew 6:19:

"Do not ever put any value on material things." Literally, you could translate this, "Lay not up for yourselves treasures on earth," but the Greek word here is *thēsauros.* Our English word *thesaurus* comes from the transliteration of this Greek word. It means a "treasure" or a "treasury of something." "Now, do not treasure earthly treasures," or we might translate it, *"Put no value on material things, which worms and rust consume and which thieves break into and steal. But you-all set your hearts on spiritual values."* Here, the same thing is used again: *"But lay up for yourselves treasures in heaven."*

Now, I don't think we're to take literally that God won't let you build up a treasure here on earth but he will let you build it up in heaven. You get that out of your head. I've read these stories about how every soul we save will be a star in our crown and we're building mansions in the sky and all like that. If the Lord won't let you have a mansion on earth, he's not going to let you have a mansion in heaven, either. He's going to be the same God. Jesus is not saying here, "Lay up for yourselves treasures in heaven, accumulate a big bank account so when you die, you can check on it for the rest of eternity." He's saying, "No, don't put any value on material things—earthly values—but you set your heart on spiritual values. They're the only real ones. For they're the ones which moths and rust cannot consume and thieves cannot break into and steal. For your values and your character are wrapped up together." He's saying that what you value and what you really are is one and the same.

We have the idea that Jesus was poor. We're told that he owned no land, no house, and no furniture. He had no automobile—he didn't even have a yoke of oxen. In fact, he had nowhere to hang his hat. He had no insurance and no Social Security. His wardrobe was the clothes he had on his back. By western standards, he was a penniless tramp—at best, a high-minded hobo. Most of us would have been embarrassed to have him as a guest in our fashionable homes, just as Zaccheus was embarrassed. Most of us would have been ashamed to acknowledge him as our friend, largely on this money matter. The most educated and successful among us would have given him free lectures about getting hold of himself, settling down in a good job, raising a family, and other free pointers on successfully conforming and adjusting to society. Perhaps some of us would have condescended and gone so far as to offer our help to him in contacting certain influential key leaders such as Caiaphus, the high priest, or Pilate the governor, with the hopes that we might get him a good job and possibly get him into the Rotary Club. We would have especially urged him to give up his messianic delusions, not to ruin himself and his future by taking such positive stands on controversial social issues.

You don't think we would have given him lectures along those lines? You bet your life we would. But now really, was Jesus poor? Well, if he was, there was really something fishy about it because he didn't have to be. He was a preacher; he came preaching. He was a teacher; he came teaching. And he was a healer, a doctor. Now, in Jesus' day, the three most highly paid professions were preaching, teaching, and healing. (Things have changed a little bit since that day.) Jesus was all three of the most highly paid professions of his day. With his preaching, he could and did attract Billy Graham crowds. He could fill any stadium any time he wanted to preach. With his teaching, he was a one-man university. And with his healing, he outdid the Mayo Clinic and Oral Roberts combined. Could you find a man today with a combination of Billy Graham and Oral Roberts and Dr. Mayo and expect to find him poor? How much was the free-will offering at Jesus' Jerusalem evangelistic crusade? What were his charges for matriculation in his classes? And how much was his bill for professional services when he healed the sick, cleansed the lepers, opened the eyes of the blind, and raised the dead? If you had a son who had actually died and a specialist so great came that he could raise him from the dead and give him back to you, you wouldn't be disappointed at any bill he sent to you, would you?

What were Jesus' bills? In spite of all of this, he died with his total possessions a rather ragged robe on his back, and the soldiers gambled for that. What was the matter with that guy? With all of his ability to be rich, he died a pauper and was buried in a borrowed grave. Something was wrong with him. His head needed examining.

No! Your head and my head need examining. He was the one who was right. Listen to him. He said, "Don't you ever put any value on these earthly possessions." I think he could have been wealthy, but he didn't want it because he saw the utter futility of striving for something that was nothing, in the final analysis, but worm food.

My daughter Eleanor used to be interested in Indian lore, and our farm is located on what was a former campground of an old tribe of Indians called "Cheehaws." We found a lot of artifacts of various kinds there and Eleanor had always been wanting to find some burial ground and one day, way down in the swamp, we were walking around and came on a great big mound of earth and she got excited and I did too, and we ran to the house and got our picks and came down there and started excavating. We had read that the Cheehaws always buried their dead near the creek. This was near the creek and it was a fairly small mound, but we were sure it would have tremendous artifacts in it, so we started digging and we were carefully pulling things away and finally, after a little while, her pick hit something hard. I knew we had struck pay dirt then and we went over and started carefully pulling the dirt away. It had a curving effect to it and we carefully unearthed it and you know what it was? It was an old fender to a Model T automobile.

Now, how in the world those Indians got it down there at all, I don't know. But the tin of the old tin lizzy was all eaten away. Rust had gotten that. But there was the big iron beam that outlined it enough to tell what it was. And as I sat there (Eleanor was ready to cry at those Indians burying a thing like that) I got to thinking.

You know, one day, that old Model T fender was a pretty nice thing. It was fastened to a nice swank automobile. And I imagined that it was owned by some college kid, only one of its kind on the campus. And he would flit around over the campus with the prettiest girl by his side, the envy of all his classmates. He was the envy of all his peers. Years passed. The rust had eaten his fender and I presume the worms had eaten him. Sooner or later, the rust and worms are going to get it all. If the rust and the worms don't beat you out, the thieves will. (They might be in the form of bankers or . . . well, I mean, they might be civilized, you know. Thieves don't always poke a pistol in your ribs. Most money is taken not with a pistol but with a pencil. You don't rob with pistols. That's barbaric. The easiest way to rob is with a pencil.)

Jesus said, "I don't want you to be money addicts. I want you to be healthy people." He explains this a little bit more. *"The body depends on the eyes for light. Now if your eyes are in focus, then the body will have clear light. But if your eyes be evil . . ."* The evil eye was supposed to be an eye that just rotated like an airport beacon. It could see in all directions. I had a schoolteacher when I was in the fourth grade that had one. She could be writing on the blackboard and see me eating a drumstick.

Jesus is saying that if your eyes are in focus on one object, then you can see clearly. But if your motives are not clear, if you're trying to be loyal to many different things and to see everything at once, the image coming in on you is so confused that you can't make heads or tails of life. The reason so many people are utterly confused this day is because their eyes are not in focus. They're trying to watch too many different things and give their loyalties to too many different things.

So then he says, *"If your eyes are not in focus, then your whole body will be in confused darkness. Now, if your light is darkness, you are really in the dark. That's why it's impossible for a man to serve two masters."* He didn't say you shouldn't; he said you can't. It's as though one might say, "No man can follow a road that forks." I can't safely say you shouldn't follow a road that forks; you just try it. I can safely say you can't. Jesus is saying here: You can't serve two masters. *"For either you will hate the one and love the other, or you will have respect for one and contempt for the other."*

It is absolutely impossible to be in bondage to both God and money. You can be in bondage to God *or* money, but you cannot be in bondage to God *and* money.

Jesus told many stories to illustrate this. One was the story of the rich farmer. You recall it in Luke. Jesus said, "There was a certain rich farmer." Now, he didn't say what the man's name was. Jesus left him rather impersonal. To make it a little bit more personal, let's give the man a name. We'll call him Sam. *"Sam's fields brought forth abundantly."* Now, we might even want to call him uncle. That would be all right, too. *"Uncle Sam's fields brought forth abundantly."* The fields brought forth so abundantly that a big committee in Washington wanted to know what he was going to do with all that wheat, cotton, potatoes, and hogs. "Oh, we'll put up a good big program of storage," he said. "We'll pull down our little barns and we'll build big ones all over the prairies of Kansas and the plains of Georgia, and there we will store our goods. These hungry folks over in China—they're all Communists anyway—let them starve to death. The only good Communist is a dead Communist. And these folks over there in India starving and crying for bread. Let them die. If they weren't so lazy, they would have plenty to eat. What they need to do is get them a good Secretary of Agriculture."

When he got it all pulled in and harvested, he said, "I say to my soul, soul, you got it made. Recline, dine, wine, and shine." And God said to him, "You nitwit. This very night, *they* are demanding your soul of you." It doesn't say, "This night your soul shall be required of you." God didn't kill that man. It's the third person plural. *"They* are demanding your soul of you." Who is "they"? All these barns, all these granaries, all these fields, all this stuff he had given himself to over the years. *They* are demanding. This guy didn't die. Something more tragic than that happened to him. He lived. He lived in bondage to the very things he thought would serve him. They demanded his soul of him.

I don't think Jesus was taking a monastic or ascetic viewpoint or attitude towards possessions. I don't think he was an ascetic. John the Baptist was, but I don't think Jesus ever shared much in John's philosophy along this line. Jesus loved the feast and the word for feast means "abundance." He loved to go to them, he loved to tell about them. I think he loved abundance, maybe because he grew up in blinding poverty, I don't know. But he was not an ascetic. On one occasion when a woman came with high-priced perfume and poured it on his feet, one of the disciples with a rather ascetic bent said, "You know, that's a waste of that perfume. Why didn't we just say, 'Well, madam, don't open it up. Don't break the seal on it. Put it in the collection plate Sunday morning and we'll trade it in.' " Jesus said, "No! Let her break it. Let her use it."

When Jesus fed the multitudes, he would start with nearly noth-

ing—with just two boxes of sardines and three boxes of saltines—
but when they got through, they picked up great big baskets of un-
eaten food of the abundance.

That isn't asceticism. Jesus never took this attitude. He took the
attitude of abundance. But at the same time, he rebuked those
people who set their eyes on possessions. It seems to me that he is
asking us to repose our lives in the greatness and goodness of God.
He says, "If you, mortal as you are, ask of your father for bread, he
surely will not give you a stone." If we ask him for bread, God will
not give us a little grudging crust. Jesus said your father is filled
with abundance. Trust him for it so that you can be free from anxiety for your own welfare; you can be free to seek the God Movement.

This is a liberating kind of thing. Jesus didn't want us shackled
by the desire for things. He's saying, "If you're going to give yourself to God as his slave, God has a responsibility in the transaction
also. For any master must provide for his slaves." God has a responsibility in the God Movement. If he's going to ask you to seek
it with singlehearted devotion, then God has an obligation to feed
and care for his slaves. And Jesus' teaching on this is that you might
be freed from it and not have to be shackled by the anxiety and
worry of providing for yourself. God will provide for you.

*Therefore, let me tell you-all something. Don't you worry about
making a living, what you'll eat and what you'll drink and what
you'll wear. Isn't the life of a man more important than what he
eats? And isn't the health of the body more important than clothing? Think for a moment about the birds of the sky. They
don't plant. They don't harvest. They don't store up in barns. Even
so, your spiritual Father cares for them. Really now, aren't you-all
more valuable than they? Besides—who of you, by fretting and
fuming, can make himself one inch taller? And what's all this big
to-do about clothing? Look yonder at that field of flowers how they
are growing. They do no housework and they do no sewing. But
I'm telling you, even Solomon in all his finery was never dressed up
like one of those flowers. Well then, if God so clothed the flowers
of the field, which are blooming today and are used for fuel tomorrow, such a fragile, valueless kind of thing—if God so lavishes all of
his artistic nature upon one little fragile, perishable rose blossom,
won't he do even more than that for you, you spiritual runts?*

What is the matter with us? Any man who ever looks at a rose
and then says, "What am I gonna wear?" is guilty of heresy and
disbelief.

So cut out your anxious talk about what are we gonna eat and what're we gonna drink and what're we gonna wear, for the people of the world go tearing around after all these things. Listen. Your spiritual Father's quite aware that you've got to have all such stuff. Then set your heart on the God Movement and its kind of life and all these things will come as a matter of course. Don't worry over the future. Let the future worry over itself. Each day has enough trouble of its own.

Now, this isn't just nice little advice that you can take or leave. I think he's setting forth here great spiritual laws of the universe —that God will provide for all who will let him. The only ones he won't provide for are those who won't let him. He'll provide for the birds. He'll provide for the flowers. He provides for everything that will let him. Jesus is setting forth a great spiritual law that operates just as certainly and as surely as the law of gravity. He says that if you'll set your heart first on the God Movement and its kind of life, and center yourself around its concepts, then he says, all of these things will come as a matter of course.

Suppose now this little lily that he was talking about or this little rose says, "You know, I don't like it out here in this field. The farmer just drove by with a manure spreader. I want to get into a better environment. The cultural opportunities are horrible out here. So I think maybe I'm going to write to my cousin in the town and see if he can't find me an apartment and I'm going to move in there." Suppose that little lily has the free will, as we have, to determine his own conduct and can move into the city and live on the concrete. Jesus is not saying to that little lily, "Take no thought about tomorrow." It had better! It won't let God take care of it; it better take care of itself. So long as it will stay in the environment which God intended for it, God will care for it. But when it wants to govern its own course, then it takes itself out of God's care.

Suppose a bird says, "You know, I don't like it way up here. It gets kinda chilly. Besides there's more to eat in the lake. I think I'm going to live in the lake." To say to a little bird that gets out of its environment and lives in another environment with its own willful desire to get into it—to say to that little bird, "Well, little bird, don't take any thought about what's going to happen to you." It had better! For it has taken itself out of the operation of God's care. It has rebelled.

This promise is given only to people who are willing to set their eyes on one object, and that is, the Kingdom of God and its righteousness. Jesus said, "You can count on it, from there on out, things will be added to you." And I can speak from experience. I believe this; I've seen it operate time and time again. In the establishment of Koinonia Farm, I remember quite well that we were supposed to pay the fellow $2500 down. Martin England, who was a missionary under the American Baptist Foreign Mission Society to Burma, and I started it together. We agreed on the common purse and I had the idea that Martin was loaded. I don't know why I should think that, he being an American Baptist missionary, but he talked about, "Let's do this and let's do that," and I said, "Yeah, let's do" and I thought he had the money. And so I said, "Let's do this and let's do that" and he said, "Yeah, let's do" and when we finally pooled our common assets, we had $57.13. We were three weeks from the time we had agreed to pay $2500 down! To make a long story short, we put down that $2500. A fellow brought it to us and said the Lord had sent him with it. I didn't question him— we took it right quick before the Lord changed his mind.

Years later, a newspaper reporter came out there and asked, "Who finances this project?"

Well, all along, folks who had helped us said that the Lord had sent them, so I said to this newspaper reporter, "The Lord does."

"Yeah," he said, "I know. But who supports it?"

I said, "The Lord."

"Yeah, I know," he said, "but who, who, who, uh, who—you know what I'm talking about. Who's back of it?"

I said, "The Lord."

He said, "But what I mean is, how do you pay your bills?"

I said, "By check."

"But," he said, "I mean—hell, don't you know what I mean?"

I said, "Yeah, friend, I know what you mean. The trouble is you don't know what I mean!"

Time and again we've had to walk right up to a door like these automatic doors that you walk up to like you're going to walk into them and it opens up just like that. We started with little or nothing and we've never missed a meal. We've had to postpone several, but I have been with it enough to know that there is an operation of a spiritual law here that is as certain as the law of gravity and I have implicit faith in it and I think it's something that we Christians need to re-examine. If we do, we're going to be on the brink of some tremendous discoveries far outweighing the discovery of atomic fission.

(EDITOR's NOTE: The following satirical translations of Scripture are from what Jordan called "the goofed-up Bible.")

And he said to them, "Take heed and beware of all unselfishness, for a man's life does consist of the abundance of his possessions." And he spake a parable unto them saying, "The ground of a certain poor man brought forth sparingly, and he thought within himself saying, 'What shall I do, for I have no way to pay all my creditors.' And he said, 'This will I do. I will consolidate all of my debts into one great debt and then I will have enough to buy a new automobile and I will say to my soul, soul, thou hast enough debts built up to last for many years. Now, thou canst moonlight, fret and worry, and have ulcers as big as anybody.' And Mammon said to him, 'Good boy, Harry. This night, thou hast become a great American. All thy debts will greatly stimulate the economy. And wilt not thy slavery enrich others?' So is he that accumulates many debts and is faithful to Mammon."

And a certain depositor asked him saying, "Good banker, what shall I do to become really rich?" And Jesus said to him, "Why callest thou me good? None is good save one—that is Mammon himself. Thou knowest the commandments, 'Do not pay fair wages,' 'Do not be honest,' 'Don't have a soft conscience,' 'Don't pay any avoidable taxes,' 'Take all the interest and profit you can get.'" And he said, "All these rules have I kept from my youth up." Now, when Jesus heard these things, he said unto him, "Yet lackest thou one thing. Sell all thou hast and put it in my bank and thou shalt have treasure on earth; and come, let me manage thy affairs." And when he heard this, he was exceedingly glad, for he himself was not much of a businessman. And when Jesus saw that he was exceedingly glad, he said, "How easily shall they who have some riches enter into the Kingdom of Mammon. For it is easier than falling off a log for an unscrupulous man to enter into the Kingdom of Mammon." And they that heard that said, "Who, then, can be poor?" And he said, "The things that are impossible with men are possible with Mammon." Then Peter said, "Lo, we have invested all and followed your advice." And he said unto them, "Verily I say unto you, there is no man that hath invested in slum houses or government bonds or suburban real estate or blue-chip securities or stocks for Mammon's sake who shall not receive manifold more dividends in this present time, and in the years ahead, everlasting status."

He moved to Jonesboro and got a job there. Now a man lived

there by the name of Zaccheus who was president of the First National Bank and was quite well off. And Jesus was anxious to meet him but had been unable to do so because there was always such a crowd waiting to see him and because Jesus himself was a very insignificant person. But one day he heard that Mr. Zaccheus was making an inspection tour of the ghetto. So he posted himself in the second-story window of his tenement, which was along the announced route. When Mr. Zaccheus got to the place where Jesus was, he looked up and saw him and told his chauffeur to stop. "Hey, boy. Hurry and come down here a minute. I'm thinking about getting out and visiting with you." So Jesus scrambled down right away and grinning from ear to ear, welcomed the rich man into his flat. When all the people saw that, they began cheering wildly. "He's actually coming inside one of our flats and visiting with us!" During the visit, Jesus said to the banker, "We gladly pay to you all these high rents and interest rates, for we are proud to be a part of this free enterprise system. We don't want to be like the Communists. So if you wish, you may double our rates, or even triple them. We shall gladly take the bread from our children to pay them." And the banker said, "Praise God for such a loyal American. This is the kind of man we like to help."

Lay up for yourselves treasures on earth where pomp and circumstance count and where friends come over to drink and flatter. But don't lay up for yourselves treasures in heaven where pomp and circumstance mean nothing, and where no friends come over to drink and lie. For where your heart is, there will your treasure be also. No man can serve two masters. For either he will hate the one and love the other or else he will hold to the one and despise the other. You cannot serve Mammon and God. Therefore I say unto you, take every precaution for your life: what ye shall eat and what ye shall drink, and especially for the body, what ye shall put on. Is not a fat bank account more than aught else, and Social Security a close second? Behold the fowls of the air, for they sow not, neither do they reap nor gather into barns—and they don't get Medicare or annuity benefits, either. Are ye any better than they? Which of you, by having faith, can make yourself one whit more miserable? And why not take thought for raiment? Consider the lilies of the field how they grow. They toil not, neither do they spin. And yet I say unto you, if Solomon in all his glory had not had a good tailor, he would have looked like a fool. Wherefore, if Solomon with his wealth and power, even though it is all passed away, was careful about his personal appearance, how much more should ye be, ye hippies? Therefore, spend all your waking hours worrying, saying, "What shall we eat and what shall we drink and wherewithal shall we be clothed?" For after all these things do the Christians seek too. Your heavenly Father knoweth that ye hath need of all these things but you can't trust him. So seek ye first the Kingdom of Mammon and its delusions, and ye shall make one grand mess of things. Take, therefore, every precaution for the future, for the future will make no provisions for you. Sufficient unto old age is the evil thereof.

THE CURRENCY OF THE KINGDOM

Don't you judge . . . (I'm going to translate this differently) *Don't you preach just to keep from being preached to.*

A lot of people enter the ministry, I think, just so they won't have to endure the pew. But now Jesus is saying: "Don't you ever enter the ministry with the view that you are going to escape the preaching that you preach. For the same sermon you preach will be applied to you. The stuff you dish out to others will be dished out to you." Every minister ought to hang that in his study. That's the meaning of this verse. He's saying the mere fact that you stand in the pulpit and tell others what to do does not release you from the responsibility of practicing what you preach. Every doctor must take his own medicine. The fact that he becomes a doctor does not give him the right to defy the laws of health; and the fact that you're a preacher does not give you the right to defy the spiritual laws. This is why Jesus never preached until first he practiced. He spoke from experience and he never preached that which he did not practice.

Why examine the splinter in your brother's eye and take no notice of the plank in your own eye. Or how can you say to your brother, "Bud, hold still while I pick that splinter outa your eye," when there's a great big plank stickin' outa yours. Listen, you phoney. First pull the plank from your eye, and then you'll be able to see better to get the splinter out of your brother's eye.

You know, it's so nice to be a splinter surgeon. If you just look around, everybody's got splinters in their eyes. I've seen folks who have two splinters in the same eye. Just everywhere you look, folks got splinters. Has it ever occurred to you that a splinter comes off a plank? The folks whom I see with splinters in their eye might have gotten their splinters off my plank. That's what Jesus is saying here.

Don't throw your valuables to the dogs, and don't spread your pearls before the hogs; or they will trample it under their feet and even turn around and bite you.

I don't know what this means, for sure. It's one of those enigmatic statements of Jesus that could mean quite a few things. He says, "Don't throw your valuables to the dogs and don't spread your pearls before the hogs." He's assuming that we have some valuables and that we have some pearls. To let them go to the dogs is to waste them. And to throw pearls to hogs symbolizes another waste.

What really are the Christian "valuables"? What are the Christian "pearls"? These pearls, these valuables, are Matthew five and six. Jesus has been pouring out his lifeblood to polish up these pearls and give them to us. Now, he's saying, don't waste them. "For heaven's sake," he's saying, "I've explained to you the mysteries of the kingdom. I have opened up this vast storehouse of God to you and I've let you go in and cram your pockets with the idea of brotherly love, with the idea of mercy, with the idea of justice. I've let you cram your pockets full of God's pearls. Now please, my friends, don't waste them. Don't bury them. Don't let them go to the dogs."

What he's saying is about the same thing he said in the parable of the talents. In that story, the master turned over some wealth to people and he said, "You-all trade with this wealth." One poor old fellow took his and wrapped it in a handkerchief and dug a hole and buried it in the earth. And the master came back and said, "Come here, boys. What have you been doing?"

One fellow said, "I've been doing business. Your ten talents have got ten more."

"Fine. That's good. You're a good fella. You'll be over ten cities. What have you been doing here, Pete?"

"Well, you didn't give me but five, but I worked with those five and I got you five more."

"Fine, fine. You'll be over five cities. Hey, Jake, how 'bout you?"

"Well, now Lord, I want to tell you something. I heard about you and I knew that you were a hardhearted man. You pick up where you don't put down. And you reap where you don't sow. Now, I know you gave me some stuff to do business with, but Lord, I was scared. I was scared of you; I was scared of everybody. I was scared of the Ku Klux Klan, I was scared of the Birchers, I was scared of the White Citizens' Council. So I took this precious money you gave me and I wrapped it up in a theological handkerchief, buried it in the baptismal pool, and covered it over with homiletical debris. Lord, I preached about it every Sunday and we sang hymns about it every Sunday. We have kept the faith, once and for all, delivered to the saints pure, undefiled, and unaugmented. Here it is, just like you gave it to Paul and Silas. Take it, Lord."

And what did the Lord of that servant say? He said, "Take it away from him! Take it away from him and give it to somebody who'll do business."

Now Jesus is saying that if he's going to turn over his pearls and his valuables to you, and you are going to waste them, it just could be that the very folks who took them away from you—that Ku Klux Klan that comes and says, "If you don't give up this business of brotherhood, we gon' kill you," and you say, "Well, well, well, don't do that. Sure, sure you can have it"—those same guys that made you surrender those treasures will turn and, with disrespect and contempt, spit in your face.

Now, I don't know. That could be what it means—that's what it ought to mean. I say that because all the seventh chapter of Matthew is exhortation. The first two chapters of the Lesson on the Mount are explanation, teaching—elaboration telling what the pearls, what the treasures are. And the final third of this man's lesson is exhortation to act on the first two-thirds.

He goes on to say that if you don't want to waste these pearls— if you really want to use them to do business—you better start asking, asking for strength, for wisdom, for insight.

Start asking and it will be given to you. Start looking and you will find. Start knocking and the door will be opened for you. For every asker receives and every seeker finds and every knocker has the door opened to him. For is there any man among you whose son shall ask him for bread and he'll give him a rock? Or if he should ask for fish, would he give him a snake? Well then, if you—weak mortals that you are—are capable of making good gifts to your children, don't you think your spiritual Father will give even better gifts to those who ask him?

These better gifts he's talking about here do not include prosperity. These better gifts are gifts to discern, to understand, to distinguish between these issues. The gift of discernment, the gift of insight, the gift of love and compassion for those who are bitterly opposing us when we try to exercise this discernment—all of these are gifts which you will absolutely have to have if you are not going to waste your pearls and your valuables. These are the gifts which the Father is quite willing to lavish upon those who are really serious about this business of exercising these treasures that he has given us in the Lesson on the Mount.

Therefore, in all of your dealings with people, treat them as you want to be treated. This, in a nutshell, is the essence of all our moral and religious principles. Approach life through the gate of discipline, for the way leading to emptiness is wide and easy and a lot of folks are taking that path. But the gate into life is hard and the road is bumpy and only a few take this route.

Keep your eye peeled for fake preachers who come to you with sheepskins from a wolf school. (This advice is to the pulpit committee.) *You'll be able to distinguish them by their ministerial tone. You'll be able to tell the difference between them by the way they live. You know, you don't gather grapes from a bramble bush nor peaches from a chinaberry, do you? So it is that a good tree makes good fruit and a bad tree makes bad fruit. It is impossible for a good tree to bear bad fruit and it is just as impossible for a bad tree to bear good fruit. Any tree that doesn't produce good fruit is chopped down and thrown into the fire. That's why I told you that you could recognize them by the way they live.*

Not everyone who glibly calls me, "Lord, Lord," shall enter the order of the Spirit. But he who does the will of my spiritual Father. The time will come when many people will gather around and say, "Lord, Lord, we sure did preach in your name, didn't we? And in your name, we sure did give the devil a run for his money, didn't we? We did all kinds of stunts in your name, didn't we, Lord?" And then I'll just have to admit right in front of everybody that I have never known you. Get away from me, you religious racketeers.

To become a church member, what do you have to do? (One friend says you have to make a monosyllabic grunt in response to a ministerial mumble.) You have to accept Jesus Christ as Lord and Savior and make a public profession of that faith. You have to say out in public, "Jesus Christ is Lord." To further signify that, you have to be baptized. You've got to say Jesus Christ is Lord and Savior in that order, for it is in his Lordship that we understand his Saviorhood. You've got to say to the whole wide world, "Jesus Christ is Lord"; and then you've got to be baptized into a fellowship that says, "Jesus Christ is Lord." So it's both an individual and group profession of faith.

Now, Jesus says that the real test of lordship is obedience to him. In the light of that, if the people who have made this public profession that Jesus is Lord were faced with a choice between Jesus and three other things—money, custom, or law—what percentage of them would choose to obey the teachings of Jesus? I assume that when we say lordship that means that we give him the right to order our lives. How many in your church membership, honestly, do you think would choose to obey Jesus? I'm assuming that the issue is laid out there as clear as it can be, that the choice is just like coming to a road that forks and you have to choose. The issue isn't always that clear, I admit. But I'm saying let's assume that it is.

(EDITOR'S NOTE: Jordan asked for a response from the audience. From a half dozen responses, the answers ranged from 0 per cent to 3 per cent.)

Now, do you see what you're saying? I'm sure you're telling me the truth, and that makes, then, the biggest lie that's being told in America, what? The biggest lie being told in America is, "Jesus Christ is Lord." It's the biggest lie that's being perpetrated. What I'm saying is, now, these people have made a public profession. They have publicly stated that Jesus Christ is Lord and have gone through baptism to say so, haven't they? But if what you've said reflects the situation all over, it means 98 per cent of the people who publicly state that Jesus Christ is Lord are lying.

That's why the man who hears these words of mine and acts on them shall be like a wise man who built his house on the rock. Down came the rain. Up rose the floods of revolution and turmoil. Out lashed the winds. They all beset that house, but it did not fall. It was on rock foundation. And the man who hears these words of mine and fails to act on them shall be like an idiot who built his house on the sand. Down came the rain. Up came the floods. Out lashed the winds. They all cut at that house and it fell and my, what a collapse.

Now, Jesus said there's only two responses, that of the wise man and that of the idiot. Let us now go forth to classify ourselves.

IV
The Distinct Identity

*"The revolution begins
with the call to be a certain kind
of person."*

METAMORPHOSIS

Jesus came preaching and all his preaching revolved around one mighty phrase. You remember when he had gone through the temptation experience it says, "And Jesus came into Galilee preaching, 'Change your whole way of thinking for the new order of the spirit is impinging upon you.'" All his preaching was to get men to go through the process of what we call "repentance," which is an awful translation of the Greek word *metanoia*.

Let me define that just a little bit. We have an English word, *metamorphosis,* which comes from that Greek word *meta,* meaning "to change," and *morphē,* meaning "form." We're familiar with that process. A little caterpillar will crawl along in the dirt and the leaves and finally the great forces of nature—the warm weather, flowers and all—begin to work changes and he climbs up on a stem and gets real still and then something great begins to happen. He begins to split open his skin and out of that little caterpillar emerges a fragile, beautiful monarch butterfly. Now this butterfly is equipped to move in the spring breezes, to go to the flowers. He's equipped with a long proboscis to reach down and get the nectar. The new order of spring has demanded that the caterpillar change his form in order to be ready for the demands and the needs that are impinging upon him. That we call *metamorphosis.*

Now, this Greek word *metanoia* is almost exactly the same word but we don't have an English word for it. It means "to go through" —not the transformation of the body, but the transformation of the mind and of the soul that equips you for a new order. It doesn't mean to "re-pent." To me, "repent" means to get all sorry for getting caught at something. This is not what *metanoia* means. It doesn't have one tiny little bit of sorrow in it. The happiest, most joyful thing you'll ever do is to *metanoia.* Would you say to the caterpillar, "Well, little caterpillar, you know I sure do feel sorry for you—you're fixin' to become a butterfly. It's terrible, man." And the little caterpillar weeps and moans and groans because he's fixing to be a butterfly. No! His birthday is here! He's about to enter into a new order that God Almighty has prepared for him. The happiest thing a little caterpillar can do is to metamorphose! And the happiest thing that can happen to a person is for the light of God to shine on him, for him to be taken out of his darkness and put in a new order of things.

Jesus says, you've got to be equipped for this new order. That little caterpillar can't reach down and get the nectar out of the flower. He can't even get up to the flower. He's got to have wings. He's got to have a different nose. He's got to have a different form. And Jesus is saying, "I'm presenting you with a new order, and you've got to have the equipment to enter into it." So the revolution begins with a call to be a certain kind of person.

Most of the time we sense that something mighty is here, but we really are afraid to get our wings. We're afraid to get our noses, for fear that somebody might chop them off. We want to stay in the old order, but we want to praise the new order. We want to stay just as I am, caterpillar and all, and don't make me any different. Most of our worship services are buzzings of the caterpillars. You seldom hear the fluttering of the wings—just the snoring of the deacons.

Jesus is saying: "I'm calling you to a thing that demands a total change of your nature so that the old things pass away. All things become new. You've got a new name. You've got a new nature. You live in a new city. You sing a new song. Everything has become new!"

You are confronted with a whole new order: Metamorphose! But why? Because the God Movement is here. It's confronting you and you must loosen your wings and fly in its freedom. You're faced with the God Movement. That's why you need to *meta-noeite.*

Now, how do you do it? Well, John answers that. Let's look at the Gospel of John, third chapter.

Now there was a man of the Pharisees, Nicodemus was his name, he was a ruler of the Jews. This man came to Jesus by night and said to him, "Rabbi . . . Reverend . . . Teacher . . . we know that you are a teacher who has come from God, for nobody can do the signs which you are doing except God be with him. (Nicodemus could interpret these signs and to him they were wonderful!) *Master, how do you do it? I don't believe anybody can do it unless God is with him," and Jesus said to him . . . "Indeed, I am telling you, except one be sired from above, he simply cannot enter the God Movement."*

Jesus did not say, "Nicodemus, you've got to be born again." He said, "You've got to be sired from above." The word he uses here is the Greek verb *gennao* which means "to set in motion the life processes." Once in a great while this verb will be used to refer to a woman giving birth. But the Greek word for "to give birth" is *tiktō,* and this is the word the Bible uses when it says

Mary gave birth to Jesus. But this word *gennao* refers not to the act of the woman, but to the act of the father. The father impregnates the woman and he begins the life processes. It refers not to the point of birth but to the point of conception. This is very important. He's talking not about a birth, but a siring. "Except a man be sired from above, he cannot enter the God Movement."

Nicodemus says to him, "How in the world can a man be sired when he's old? When he's already been sired! I don't catch it. Can he go back into his mother's womb again, and there be sired?"

He was saying, "Can you unravel a man and take him all the way back to the point of conception? Are you saying that's what *metanoia* is? I don't get it!" Jesus is talking about being sired from above. Nicodemus is saying he's already been sired.

Jesus said to him: "I want to tell you, except one be sired out of water and out of spirit, he can't enter the God Movement."

What's this siring out of water and siring out of spirit? What's this *water!* Baptism? No! If it was, you'd have to raise the question about immersion or sprinkling. You would get all bogged down. He's not talking about baptism. What's this *water?* The Word of God? No, that's not this water. The Word of God would be spirit. Read it a little bit further:

Except a man be sired out of both water and spirit, he can't enter the God Movement. That which is sired out of flesh, that is flesh. That which is sired out of spirit, that is spirit.

This *water* is fluid. This refers not to the fluid of birth, but the fluid of conception—semen. It's a fluid (seminal fluid) in which life is resident. There is no fluid that has life in it except semen.

Jesus is simply saying here that just as your physical life is the result of the union of two forms of life, so is your spiritual life. You can't automatically sire yourself spiritually any more than you can sire yourself physically. You've got to have fluid in which life is resident in order to have life. A woman could read every page of the Kinsey Report and never become pregnant. There's got to be that which has life in it, that which can give life. He's saying here that a spiritual life cannot automatically be generated any more than physical life. That which is sired out of semen, that is flesh. That which is sired out of spirit, that is spirit.

"Don't marvel that I'm telling you that you must be sired from above. The spirit-wind blows where it wants to and you hear the sound of it, but you don't know where it comes from nor where

*it goes. That's the way it is with one that is sired out of spirit."
Nicodemus answered and said to him, "How in the world can
this be?" And Jesus said to him, "Are you a professor of Israel,
and you don't understand these things? What we have seen we're
testifying to, and you won't receive our witness. If I have told
you earthly things and you don't catch on, how would you ever
catch it if I told you spiritual things?"*

Jesus is saying, "Nicodemus, here you are, professor at the seminary, and I have told you a little physical example of birth. You
don't even catch on to that. What if I had just spouted pure theology? You'd really had a rough time of it, professor." He goes
on to say in verse 16: "For God so loved the world (that is, God
loved the world just as a husband loves a wife) that he gave his
only begotten (This verb in the Greek can be either active or passive. You can translate it "only begotten" or "only begetting" and
be correct either way.) so that whoever believes on him, or receives him (like an infertilized egg receives sperm) might not
perish away (like an infertile egg perishes) but that it might have
spiritual life."

The egg without God perishes. God without man in a sense
perishes in that he is unfulfilled. Man is as necessary to God as
God is to man, just as the egg is as necessary to the sperm as the
sperm is to the egg. Either one, apart from the other, is unfulfilled.
But when you get them together you've got spiritual life! Then
you've got this *metanoia*—this newness of life.

JESUS CHRIST REVEALED

This letter (called I Peter) is from the fellow who was the closest
to Jesus, perhaps, than any other human being. This is from Rock
Johnson, who said he was on the mountain with Jesus and heard
a voice coming out of the sky saying, "This is my Son. Y'all listen
to him." And Rock is trying to get his hearers to listen to Jesus,
to obey him.

That word *listen* means "to listen with a response of obedience."
Like my mama used to say to me sometimes when I was a kid,
"You *listen* to me!" I knew what that meant. It didn't mean just
hear what she said. It meant to *do* what she said. And when she
said, "Clarence, did you hear me?" I knew she wasn't talking
about a response with my ears. She wanted to see a response of
obedience. And so Rock said, "I was on the mountain with him,
and I heard a voice saying, 'This is my Son. Y'all listen to him.' "

I think we can say this letter is from Rock Johnson. The thing that bothers a lot of the scholars is that this is perhaps the most educated Greek in all the New Testament outside of the Letter to the Hebrews. It's the work of a scholar, of a man who is well trained, a man who knew how to use words—big words—and many scholars say that's the reason it couldn't have been written by Rock Johnson, who was an uneducated old fisherman. But I'm not too sure that Rock Johnson was so uneducated. I venture to say he had his master's degree in fishing and perhaps was writing his Ph.D. on the coloration in the iris of the eye of the pink-eye salmon or some such enlightening thing like that. Perhaps he was getting his Ph.D. in ichthyology from the fishing school over there at Capernaum or some of those other places. I'm not too sure that he was an ignorant man. Furthermore, Rock himself said that he had dictated it to Silas. Now, in those days, when you dictated a letter, your secretary had the right to put it in his own words. Paul did a lot of his dictating to Silas. I venture to say that Professor Silas touched this letter up considerably before it was read at the First Baptist Church in Pontus. So maybe Professor Silas touched it up, but it's Peter's thoughts. It might not be Peter's language, but it's Peter's thoughts.

Now, let's get into it. He identifies himself immediately. In those days you didn't sign a letter, you began it with your name so folks didn't have to look at the last of your letter to see who it was from before they started reading it. Rock calls himself an apostle of Jesus Christ. "Apostle" comes from the Greek word *apo,* meaning "from," and *stellō* meaning "sent out." It means one who's sent out from or by someone. It's about the equivalent of our word *agent,* one who has been entrusted with power, with a message, with a job, and Rock is calling himself the agent of Jesus Christ. Jesus has entrusted him with a mission, and he's been sent on a mission for Jesus Christ. Now, to whom is he writing? He says, "I'm writing to the elect sojourners—(the word here in the Greek means "a pilgrim" or "a wanderer, a migrant") to the migrant Christians who are scattered around in Florida, Georgia, Oklahoma, Texas, and California," he would be saying today.

He called them migrants, wanderers, sojourners, pilgrims, not because this earth was not their home. It was. This earth is the Christian's home. You don't go home when you die. You are already at home. It wasn't a geographical change of location that he was talking about here. This migrancy, this strangeness is not that some day we shall die and someone else will live in our house and sit in our chair and read our books and we shall be remembered no more. This is not it. The migrant, the sojourner, is one who is a stranger to the well-ordered communities of this earth. He's a stranger because his ideas are strange and foreign. He's a stranger because he's a new creature. His life is on new foundations. He's got new motivations, new valuations, a new outlook. He's a stranger in the council halls of the wicked. He has caught a glimpse of brother love and he's a stranger at a Ku Klux Klan meeting. He isn't at home there. He has caught a vision of a world of sharing and he isn't at home in the halls of finance and big business. That's not his land. He's a stranger. Rock is talking here about being a stranger to the world and its affairs. The real home of the Christian is this earth, under the spirit and guidance and influence of Jesus Christ. So he's writing to pilgrims, elect chosen pilgrims, who are scattered through Pontus, Galatia, Cappadocia, Asia, and Bithynia.

They are pilgrims according to the *fore-knowledge*. They translate this. In the Greek it's *prognōsis*. Our English word *prognosis* comes from this. A *prognosis* is when a doctor tries to diagnose what the trouble is, and then, in the light of that trouble and in the light of his resources, to determine what the probable outcome will be. Now, God has made a prognosis of this earth. He has looked at it, he has diagnosed it as sick and going to hell. But is this God's prognosis? Well, not if he can have some pilgrims to scatter around in this old sick world. Just as a doctor might make a prognosis of death from a disease if he doesn't have an antibiotic. But, the doctor might say, if I can get such and such a medicine and get it here in time, my prognosis is quite different. This patient will live.

This is what Rock is saying. God has diagnosed the earth, but he's got to have some medicine, he's got to have some people through whom he can give it. That's who these selected pilgrims are. They are God's medicine for this world. He isn't saying, "I want you all to die and come up here with me." He's saying, "I want you to live and work among those people so my prognosis of this world will come out right." And what's his prognosis? Salvation. But God Almighty can't save the world without his antibiotics and we are his antibiotics.

He's got to have us in this world, but not *of* this world. We must be in the world. We must love the world, for God loved the world. We must preach to the world. We must teach the world. We must heal the world. There is only one thing we can't do and that's make our peace with the world. The moment we do and form an alliance with it, the Spirit of God departs from us. So, then, the saints, the sanctified, the pilgrims, are those who are willing to be set apart by God's spirit.

Now, Rock says, *"Three cheers for the Father-God of our Lord Jesus Christ! By his overflowing mercy he has refathered us into a life of hope, based on the raising of Jesus Christ from the dead."* Rock is saying we are pilgrims, we are sojourners because we are a different breed. We have a unique Father. We've been re-sired. If we are sons of God, we are of a different breed.

Rock said, *"We've been re-sired into a life of hope, based on the raising of Jesus Christ from the dead."*

Now, this raising of Jesus Christ from the dead was not to guarantee our immortality. It was to guarantee our spirituality, our refathering into a new life—newness of life, Paul called it. And this raising of Jesus Christ from the dead was but the Father's final vindication of the kind of life that Jesus lived, the kind of spirit that he had, and the Father saying, *"This* spirit will live on this earth." Rock is saying here that if God Almighty can break the bonds of death in all of its aspects for his son Jesus Christ, then surely he can break the bonds of death that shackle us and make us slaves to sin and selfishness and greed in this old world, and re-sire us that we may be born as sons of God.

"This gave us (or put us) in an inheritance that's unbroken, uncorrupted and undwindling—a spiritual family set up especially for you who are sheltered by God's power. This power is yours because of your faith in the solution that's ready to be made crystal clear in the last time (or the last season)."

We think of that as referring to the Second Coming and the Final Judgment. No, this isn't what he's saying at all. The final showdown is whenever Christians confront the forces and powers of this world. The end of the world is the beginning of the kingdom, just as the end of darkness is the beginning of light. Wherever light and darkness come in conflict, that's the showdown. Whether it's in this age or that generation is immaterial. It's when light and darkness are conflicting—that's the final age, that's the showdown. When the Christians were talking about Jesus coming and ushering in the end of the world, they weren't talking about the cataclysmic windup of this physical world. They were talking about the coming of light, a dawn that's coming in the hearts of men.

I have seen this wherever brotherhood is preached. One of the reasons I think that some of the plantation owners had it in so hot for us at Koinonia Farm was because they saw, in the kind of life that we were proclaiming, the end of their world. It was the end of their plantation system, the end of their exploitation. Wherever brotherhood comes in, that's the end of the world for exploitation and arrogance. This final showdown is any showdown between the forces of Jesus Christ and the forces of evil.

Delight in this, that you are a part of this showdown, even though for a while it is necessary for you to put up with all kinds of harassment.

When? When you die? No. Now! This life is a life of conflict and you'll be harassed with all kinds of harassment.

But when your faith is tested like this, it will be more valuable than perishable gold which is also tested by fire. And at a clear presentation of Jesus Christ, your faith stands out with commendation, genuineness and respect.

They translate this in the King James, "that you might be found unto praise and honor and glory at the appearing of Jesus Christ." Now, when is the appearing of Jesus Christ? The Greek word is *apokalupsis*. It's from *apo* meaning "off" and *kaluptō* meaning "a veil." So this passage refers to the unveiling of Jesus Christ. When you have this faith that he's talking about, then it will shine through with great illumination at the unveiling of Jesus Christ. When is this unveiling of Jesus Christ? When is this revelation of Jesus Christ? It's when a soul with the spirit of Jesus in him stands up and remains true to his Lord. That's Jesus Christ revealed.

When my daughter Jan graduated from high school, she sent out invitations to all her friends in Americus, Georgia, without regard to color and one of her friends was a young Negro man that was working on the farm with us. He went and we were turned away at the gate and so she didn't graduate. She sat up in the stands and watched the graduation. This was one time, I think, that she really didn't want to be a pilgrim. I think she wanted to sit in the graduating class. The graduates were lined up under the stands at the stadium, ready to march out. But when they wouldn't let her friends, who were of a different color, come, she got out of the line in her cap and gown and she went up to the front of the line and told the assistant principal: "Sir, I think my friends have just as much right to see my graduation as anybody else's friends." He said, "Well . . . uh . . . well . . . uh . . . well . . . uh." While he was standing there saying "well-uh," Jan headed over toward the stands where the audience was sitting. She walked over to the stands, with about 3000 people looking at her in her cap and gown, climbed up to the top, and sat down to watch the procession. An honors student made a speech on moral responsibility and another student made a speech on reverence for God and man, and Jan was sitting up there in the stands in her cap and gown. Her name was never called. She never received her diploma. She was a pilgrim, a sojourner, and, I must confess, that night with her white cap and gown on I was real proud of her. She looked like an angel sojourner to me. She was feeling the sting of the pilgrimage, of being a sojourner in a strange land.

Rock continues by saying, *"You are indescribably happy with one whom you've never seen but still love, whom you've never caught a glimpse of, but still have faith to live by."* This pilgrimage is a difficult kind of thing, but when you begin to consider the alternatives, then you realize that this pilgrimage is a happy kind of thing. You don't get the feeling that you're being persecuted and rejected. You rejoice that you have this opportunity to be a pilgrim, to bear the message.

As a result of a faith like that, you'll find the answer to your deepest needs. In fact, this is the solution that was sought after and studied over by the old-time preachers who foresaw the undeserved favor that would fall on you. Under the leadership of the spirit of Christ that was in them, they studied hard to find out who would have the credentials of the suffering Christ and when he would appear. And it was made clear that the matters they were dealing with were not for them but for you. These very things are now explained to you by those who, in the Holy Spirit from on high, brought the Good News to you. They are things of which angels themselves have a craving to be a part.

He says this business of being a pilgrim is about the highest honor that can ever come to a person, that the old-time prophets pored over their scriptures trying to learn what the gospel message would be, how it would come about, and they weren't able to get it. I can see the old fellows now, poring over the scriptures—"What does this mean, what does that mean?" What they wouldn't have given for somebody to have interpreted it to them. This is a great priceless inheritance that we have to be sired into the family of God.

He says, "Folks, don't think this is something the Supreme Court handed down and you've got to comply with. This is something that God in his great mercy and kindness and love gave you. You should consider it a privilege. You didn't get this on your own.

It was God's free gift. When this prejudice has been breathed into you since infancy, you don't get rid of it easily. It takes a divine intervention."

Now, as I translate this next passage I'm going to have to localize it in a given situation and I shall have to date it. In doing so I shall not be doing violence to the spirit of the New Testament, which was a local book written in a dated period of time. It is only as the Word becomes flesh and lives among us in our time and in our space that the Word becomes alive to us. The words that Paul used in speaking to his hearers were words that were alive to them, words that had tremendous connotations. So the work of the translator is to find words that will as nearly as possible convey the idea in the present contemporary setting that these words conveyed in a setting long ago.

The word that gives me the most trouble is this Greek word *ethnē*. Our English word *ethnic* comes from it. It means "races" or, as it is always translated in the Revised Standard, "gentiles." The Jews divided the world under two headings: Jews and Gentiles. They had a subheading under Jews which was Samaritans. But they got rid of those real quick. They just had no dealings with those at all. In the Jew's mind, anybody who was not a Jew was a Gentile. Later the Church came to give the same meaning to anybody who was not in the church membership—he was a Gentile. So it has both of these connotations. I can't find an exact equivalent but since I am making a Koinonia Cotton Patch translation of the Scriptures, I'm going to translate it from the Georgia cotton patch. This is what *"wherefore,"* Rock says. Whenever he starts preaching he comes around to his "wherefore"—that's the hard rock-part of his message. You can get along with the teachings, but when it comes around to the "wherefore," you better perk up your ears. King James's translation is: *"Wherefore, gird up the loins of your minds, be sober and hope to the end for the grace that is to be brought unto you at the revelation of Jesus Christ."*

I hope you understand what that means. Here's what he's saying: "So then, put work clothes on your mind." Now wait a minute. We don't want work clothes. We're talking about an inheritance reserved in the heavens. Put a shroud on us. Don't put work clothes on us. Put a shroud on us, so we can go to our eternal reward. Rock says, "Uh-uh. You ain't dead yet. Get your blue jeans, Bubba. Don't you come here to me with a shroud. You get your blue jeans, there's work to be done. Put work clothes on your mind." Oh, not work clothes. Let us put worship clothes on. Let us put on our new robes that we just bought, our choir robes, and we'll sing glory to thy name. Lord, don't talk to us about blue jeans. Can't you let us have some choir robes? Or, Lord, now listen. You know, a preacher ain't supposed to wear blue jeans. How about clerical garb? Wherefore, get your worship clothes and preach a sermon? No, Rock says, "Get your blue jeans and get moving."

"Have a grown man's hope in the spiritual power that's delivered to you as a clear presentation of Jesus Christ."

Again we're saying that this clear presentation, this revelation, is an unveiling of Jesus Christ. That is, when people have his glory in their faces, people look upon them and say, "There is Jesus Christ. I see Jesus in these people." It is said that the believers were first called Christ-ians at Antioch, perhaps because people saw in them the image of Christ, and this was an unveiling of Jesus Christ. This is actually what Rock said at Pentecost when he tried to say that this Jesus whom you killed is now alive again. Pentecost was an unveiling, a revelation of Jesus Christ.

You can look through all of the Book of Acts and you never find the apostles citing the empty tomb as evidence of the resurrection of Jesus. The resurrection of Jesus was the core of all their preaching, but they never tried to back it up by saying, "The tomb was empty. We ourselves went there and saw it was empty and the stone was rolled away." True, the tomb was empty. True, the stone was rolled away. But the evidence of the resurrection was not the empty tomb; it was the spirit-filled fellowship. They cited *themselves* as the evidence of the resurrection. They were the new body of Jesus Christ. They were his face, his hands. They were the revelation—the resurrected body of Jesus Christ.

Now that you are God's obedient children, don't be controlled by the hankerings you had before you saw the light. Instead, you should be different in your whole manner of life, just as he who invited you to it is different. For there's a verse which says, "You all be different, because I am different."

THE MIND OF CHRIST IN THE RACIAL CONFLICT

The racial conflict is by far the most widespread, the most damaging to life, property and soul, the most unresolvable of all the conflicts which beset mankind. War, as horrible and as agonizing as it is, is more confined geographically—at least up to now—and is generally of less duration. War is devastating like a tornado, but it is not as widespread or as timeless as the racial conflict. The racial conflict is global and seemingly eternal. In the midst of this raging conflict, so destructive of life and of property and of soul, most Americans are seeking the mind of the President and not the mind of Jesus Christ. They look to the decisions of the Supreme Court, not to the dictates of the Sermon on the Mount. We listen only to law, and spurn grace. We act from compulsion, and walk not in the ways of love.

Such an approach may make our lives tolerable, but not enjoyable. Where, then, is the answer? After many years of involvement in the racial conflict, I am more convinced now than ever that the answer lies not in government nor in law, but in God and in grace. Nowhere do we see an answer more clearly than in the person of Jesus Christ of Nazareth. The answer, then, lies in seeking the mind of Jesus Christ, and not only seeking his mind but acting upon it. Finding the mind of Jesus is not difficult, for on no other subject was Our Lord more specific, more outspoken, more challenging, and more rebuking. For three years he taught by parable, precept, and practice the Father's love for the people of the whole world. The parables of the Good Samaritan, of Lazarus and Dives, the Prodigal Son, the Lost Sheep, the Lost Coin, the Great Feast—all these speak of the Father's universal love. Through his own action he demonstrated that God loved all mankind. When others were separating themselves from the Samaritans, he had to go through Samaria—not because the roads were better that way, but because he could not accept the traditions of the world which excluded the Samaritans. He had to go through Samaria in order to keep his Saviorhood of all mankind intact.

While going through Samaria he surprised a woman of another race by asking her for a drink of water. And she said, "How is it that you, a Jew, are asking drink of me, a Samaritan?" And one of the most delightful discourses in all the Gospels takes place when Jesus steps across racial boundaries. His sharpest words were reserved for a group of people called *pharisees.* The word *pharisee* is not synonymous with the word *hypocrite,* contrary to what we may think. You know what the Hebrew word *pharisee* means? It'll surprise you. It means "a segregationist"; it means "one who separates himself." "Woe unto you, segregationist!" And if we translate it as it should be translated, I think a lot of Southern Christians might join Buddhism or some other religion. "Woe unto the segregationists!"

So it is not difficult to discover the mind of Christ. I find it difficult to implement the mind of Christ.

Let's take up Ephesians, chapter two, where Paul digs into this race problem. We must bear in mind that the Apostle Paul was living in a time that was more turbulent with racial dissension and discord than even ours is. It was a time when Jews had no dealings with Samaritans and Gentiles; it was a time when Greeks had no dealings with barbarians. The whole civilized world was boiling with racial antipathies and prejudices. The Christian faith could not keep silence in the midst of problems of that nature and so we naturally expect Paul to write to the churches about this urgent and pressing problem which was facing them. He did not feel that they should wait until the storm broke over their heads in order to find some answer. They should be tackling it at the moment and trying to find the mind of Christ.

In days gone by (that is, before you ever heard the Christian Gospel) *you all were living in your sin and filth like a bunch of stinking corpses, giving your allegiance to material things and ruled by the power of custom.*

This sin and filth that Paul was talking about was their pride and arrogance and their prejudice. It wasn't their smoking and their solitare and their dancing. It was these terrible things, like pride and money-grabbing and prejudice. And he said, "You were living in it because you were giving your allegiance to material things and you were ruled by the power of custom." These are the two taproots of prejudice—material things and custom. This is why I've never allowed myself to possess anything. The moment you begin to own something you become vulnerable in trying to protect it. You know why the liberation movement in the South is being led largely by children and college students? It's because they're less vulnerable economically.

You all can still see this spirit (this spirit of materialism and custom) *working now in the lives of those who won't listen. In fact at one time or another, all of us were following our selfish inclinations and doing just as we pretty well pleased because we were naturally just as big scoundrels as everybody else. But even though we were a bunch of corpses rotting in our mess, God in his overflowing sympathy and great love breathed the same new life into us as into Christ. (You have been rescued, I remind you, by Divine Intervention.)*

Now, you see how Paul is tackling this race problem. He isn't saying, "Well, you know the Supreme Court is done said y'all got to integrate, and it's coming sooner or later so, dadgum it, I guess we might as well start integrating. Poor us." That isn't a Christian approach at all. Paul says "You're like a bunch of rotten corpses that weren't even embalmed and you were stinking to high heaven and God when he passed over you smelled the stink, and decided to do something about it and instead of just bulldozing you off into a common grave, he decided to raise you from the dead and give you some new life. And instead of accepting this idea begrudgingly you ought to thank God that you're alive and that you're no longer a stinking corpse; that you've been freed from these old prejudices and these old hates that blight your life and tear you apart, and a new life has been breathed into you by the Almighty God." That's what Paul's talking about.

"By grace you have been saved." I translate *saved* as "be rescued." If a man is in the ocean sinking and he says "Save me, save me!" we don't go quote a verse of Scripture to that guy. We get him out. This is what Paul's talking about—"being saved." It means to be rescued, to be pulled out of this mess, and cleaned up and put in to something new.

You have been rescued, I want to remind you, by Divine Intervention. With Christ, he resurrected us and elevated us to the spiritual household. All of this so clearly demonstrates forever the untold richness of his favor which he so kindly bestowed on us in Christ Jesus. So again I remind you, you have been rescued by his kind action alone, channeled through your faith. You didn't get this on your own. It was God's free gift.

Paul would've said, if he'd a been a cotton picker:

So, then, always remember that previously you Negroes, who sometimes are even called niggers by thoughtless white church members, were at one time outside the Christian fellowship, denied your rights as fellow believers, and treated as though the gospel didn't apply to you, hopeless and God-forsaken in the eyes of the world. Now, however, because of Christ's supreme sacrifice, you who once were so segregated are warmly welcomed into the Christian fellowship.

See the difference that Christ makes? Paul wants to make it crystal clear to these churches that if they take up this idea of dragging somebody out of their fellowship because he comes in with the wrong color of skin, they're dead wrong. They are not only sub-Christians, they are non-Christian. That's a strong statement, but I think the Apostle Paul will bear it out. If there are no middle walls of partition in God's house, how can there be in his

Church? Any church or any person who erects these barriers of race or external differences is guilty of the worst kind of heresy and should no longer consider himself a member of God's family.

Paul continues: *"He himself is our peace."* You see how Paul keeps arguing this race question? Not from the economic standpoint, because the big Wall Street guys could beat him on that. He didn't argue it from the standpoint of, "Well, now we got to be nice to these people because science proves that there's no difference between men." He never resorted to arguments like that. He always kept coming back and reminding these people that, first and foremost and above everything else, your commitment is to Jesus Christ.

Now I have tackled many prejudiced Southern people in my lifetime, and I have been ousted in many arguments, but I've never had one to beat me in this argument that Jesus Christ teaches that in his family men are brothers. This is really the reason why I studied Greek. It wasn't to impress anybody with a little bit of learning. That isn't the reason I studied Greek. I knew that I was going into the Southland to give my life to the Lord and I knew that I would be coming into contact with a lot of people, both clergy and laity, who claimed to be followers of Jesus Christ, and I wanted to know what the man was saying. I didn't want some little jackleg preacher tying me up in knots because I didn't know what my Lord said. And I rooted myself in the Greek language that I might understand, and I think by God's grace I do understand, at least this little part of Ephesians here.

He himself is our peace; it was he who integrated us. And abolished the segregation patterns which caused so much hostility.

The thing that just burns my heart out and that I can hardly bear is that the Supreme Court is making more pagans be Christian than the Bible is making Christians be Christian. I can hardly take it at times when the whole integration struggle is being fought, not in the household of God, but in the bus depots, sitting around Woolworth's counter, arguing over whether you can eat hamburger and drink Cokes together, when we ought to be sitting around Jesus' table drinking wine and eating bread together. It just burns me up that we Christians with the word of God in our hearts have to be forced to sit around Woolworth's table and that we still segregate Christ's table. The sit-ins would never have been necessary if the Christians had been sitting down together in church and at Christ's table these many years. If anybody has to bear the blame and guilt for all the sit-ins and all the demonstrations and all the disorder in the South, it is the whitewashed

Christians who have had the word of God and have locked it up in their hearts and refused to do battle with it.

I think the world is looking for a new church building. I've been around and looked at so much of this beautiful church art and modern architecture. I was up North a while back in a big city and the pastor took me around and showed me a big church house that cost a million dollars. It was one of these graceful swooping things that went up into a big, beautiful cross way up on top and he pointed to it and he said, "Even our cross cost us $10,000." And I said, "Brother, you got gypped. The time was you could get them for nothing."

I don't think the world is looking for any modern architecture. It's looking for a fellowship of people who've learned the secret revealed to them by the grace of God that they can live together in peace and harmony.

It is for this reason—that is, my Christian convictions on race— that I, Paul, am now in jail. (I suppose you heard about my assignment on your behalf which, by God's grace, was given to me.) The secret was made known to me by a revelation, about which I briefly wrote before. If you will reread it, you'll clearly understand my insight into this secret of Christ's. You'll also find that it was not made known to the people of former times as now it has been made crystal clear to his dedicated preachers and deeply spiritual men of God.

When Paul has been let in on this "secret" that people of another race are included in God's plan of the ages, it begins to have some effect on him. He has to do something about it and he winds up in the clink. It was not that he couldn't have escaped it. He could have. He had three alternatives opened to him. He could have rejected it. He could have said, "Well, after all, human beings are human beings. We've got our sacred Southern way of life and we've got to keep it." He could have identified himself with the culture and wound up with a pretty big place of influence. And he would never have risen to anything else for fear of losing that influence.

Time and again I have seen men stand in the pulpit and do away with the very teachings of Jesus on the grounds that they are trying to keep their "influence." If they were perfectly honest they would perhaps admit that they were less concerned about their influence than they were about their affluence. A man who has not taken his stand on the gospel is in danger of not having much influence anyway for the Christian faith.

Or Paul could have taken a middle-of-the-road position. He could've said, "Sure, God has included the Gentile, but you know it's going to take time and I'm pushing on this thing in my way, and we'll all kind of push along together, and in time things will be solved." If he had taken this position, he would really have been in prison. I know of no one more miserable today than the moderates in the South. They're trying to hold a position that is absolutely untenable—the middle-of-the-road position. When you straddle the fence you are respected by neither side and you are capable of leading neither side. As the writer of the Hebrew says, "The word of God is as sharp as a two-edged sword, cutting down to the dividing of the joints even to the marrow of the bone." Now, that means that the Word of God is razor sharp, and when you try to straddle it, you get cut; you get in great agony.

So Paul says, "It is for this reason—my own Christian convictions on race—that I, Paul, am now in jail."

It was his third alternative and really the only one open to him. You recall how he happened to be in jail. He wasn't in the Roman prison on a two-year sabbatical doing a doctoral thesis on the Roman penology. It wasn't that. He had gone down there to Jerusalem and taken with him one of his converts and that convert happened to be a little off-color—I mean skin color. He was an Ephesian—Trothemus the Ephesian. And Paul was seen in one of the local cafés eating with him. And they thought that because he was eating with him he was going to church with him.

Now it's one thing to have a sit-in in the cafeteria. It's *another* thing to have a sit-in in the church. And when they saw him walking down the street they knew he and this Ephesian were heading toward the First Baptist Church. And it was more than they could take. They didn't wait for him to walk up the steps. They knew his position on race. It had been made clear to them and they knew when he walked down the street with this Ephesian that he was going to church with him and this was going to be a demonstration as to whether or not the church would accept this Ephesian. Well, they set up this big tumult and finally the cops came running and wanted to know what was going on. And they saw this little weak fellow down on the ground with everybody beating him and kicking him and spitting on him—an awful place for a preacher to be —but that's where Paul was.

Finally the Roman soldier grabbed him by the collar and said, "What's going on here, boy?" And Paul said, "Let me talk to the people." When he spoke in Greek, the Roman official said, "Why,

I thought you were that insurrectionist that was stirring up all this trouble. I thought you were one of those outside agitators." And Paul said, "Why, no, I'm not. I want to speak to the people." And so they let him talk to the people and Paul told about a revelation that was given to him to preach the Word to the Gentiles, "the Negroes." And when he said that, somebody hollered for the tar and feathers, and Paul had to be taken into the prison to be protected. He was taken into protective custody. And when they were going to beat him to find out what his defense was, Paul said, "Is it lawful to beat a Roman citizen?" And it just scared the life out of them and they went running to the chief of police and said, "You know, we got the wrong possum in this trap!" Paul was given the semblance of a trial, but he appealed to the Supreme Court and now he's in Rome waiting for his case to come up before the Supreme Court. And that's what he's doing in jail—because of his convictions on race.

Now let's don't feel sorry for Paul. I know this is not a good place for a preacher to be, but let's don't feel sorry for him. You know, today when we call a man to a church we investigate the years he's spent in the seminary. We want to know whether he can be all things to all men—sort of an executive, a psychologist, a counselor, a businessman of all kinds, a public relations man. Actually, we're looking more for an octopus from the seminary than we are a prophet from God. I think we ought to begin to investigate not so much how many years he's spent in the seminary diddling around on a doctoral thesis, but how many years he's spent in jail, because somehow or other a man is better able to get up a sermon in a cell than he is in a church study.

Paul goes on to say in verse six: *"The secret* (that is, the secret that was made known to me by revelation) *is that Gentiles* (or the Negroes) *are fellow partners and* equal *members, co-sharers in the Gospel of Jesus Christ. As a result of God's kindness, so freely bestowed on me and so undeserved, I am now an ardent advocate of that Gospel."*

Prison instead of silencing Paul had made him all the more convinced of the rightness of his position. And then he says this: *"I just can't get over it that I, the least likely of all the Christians, was chosen for this honor—the honor of explaining to the Negroes the untapped resources of Christ, and to make clear to them what their part is in this insight that God created everybody alike, but which has been so little understood in the past."* You see what a great honor he's considering it to be? It was an honor to be caught up in this conflict. No Supreme Court was ramming this down his throat.

It was a glorious privilege, a wonderful secret that he was let in on and which he wishes to share with the world.

"Today God's richly colored wisdom has been gotten over to the authorities and the leaders in high places by the action of the church." Who was out there in the forefront of this integration movement in Paul's day? Oh, we know. It was the NAACP. Let me give you a little of the alphabet that's in the forefront in the South today: NAACP, CORE, SNCC, SCLC, ACLU. How long will it be before another bit of the alphabet will be added, CHURCH?

This is in accordance with His eternal intent which He expressed in Christ Jesus our Lord. In him we have the boldness and the confidence to give such an expression to our faith. And when I think of all of this I get down on my knees before the Father who has stamped his image on every race in heaven and on earth, and I beg him to give you, out of his glorious abundance, the power to win by his spirit, ruling your inner life. God grant that Christ, through your faith, might establish residence in your hearts.

MAKING A HABIT OF LOVE

With chapter three of the Book of Ephesians, Paul ends the theological and sociological parts of his letter. For the next three chapters he deals with personal problems and personal relations. We might call the first part the "social gospel" and the second part the "personal gospel." This is as it should be. I've noticed in my experience that many times we people who put so much emphasis on the social aspects of the gospel are frequently trying to dodge some of its personal demands. We at Koinonia have been so *adept* at solving the national problems and so *inept* at solving our neighbor problems. We are much more skilled in telling the nations how to get along with each other than we are in getting along with each other in our own fellowship. And it has also been my observation that many times people, particularly young people, who are so anxious to "do something" about the race problem, to create harmony between the races, are using that as a cover-up for some deep, inner conflict within themselves. And I deal gently here, for I consider myself in the group who advocate world peace and nonviolence and pacifism. But so frequently those of us who so ardently advocate pacifism are using it as a cover-up for the great hostilities that are seething within our own hearts. So it is wise and right that Paul should use at least half his letter to deal with the direct, specific personal application of the faith of Jesus Christ.

Let's pick it up with him in the fifth chapter:

"Therefore, become God's mimics, like children who are dearly loved." His exhortation here is to mimic God as dearly beloved children. The big thing that God is doing is loving. And this imitation of God is to take on the Godlike life that humbles itself and gives itself to mankind. God is not an example, but a Savior, and it is this saving, loving action which we are to imitate. I have observed a lot of children in my life and I seldom, if ever, have noticed one mimic someone he does not love, or someone who does not dearly love him. He will mimic his father if he really loves him. A little girl will imitate her mother. Seldom will a child imitate one whom he feels has a feeling of hostility. So Paul is saying, be God's mimics, as children in a relationship of love.

Then he goes on to say, *"Make love a habit."* And here's where he's saying that the real imitation of God is loving him:

Make love a habit, just as Christ loved you and gave himself up for us as an offering and sacrifice to God like a fragrant perfume. Don't let sexual sins or any kind of lewdness or moneygrubbing even be mentioned among you, just as Christians ought to behave.

This word *moneygrubbing* means to go to an excess, not just in money, but in everything. It means to go too far. Paul could be applying this not to just money but to all things—sex and lewdness and money and drinking, etc.

This should be absolutely clear to you, that anybody who is sexually loose, or a punk or a moneygrubber, has no place in God's and Christ's spiritual family.

I think it's kind of strange that Paul would put greed along with sexual license. These fine, wealthy aristocratic Christians who look down their noses at a prostitute don't realize that God is putting them in the same category with the prostitutes. Back in the days of Paul, for a man to get drunk on money was as terrible a sin as to get drunk on alcohol, or to run around with loose women. Times have changed a little bit since then. We don't put a man that's drunk with money out of the church today. We make him a deacon —that is, if he tithes.

Don't let anybody kid you with slick talk. That's why God is mad at the people who've gone to the dogs. Don't let 'em suck you in. For you once operated under cover of darkness, but now in the Lord's light behave as people of light. For light produces only goodness and uprightness and truth. Behave as people of light.

Don't ever join an organization that has to operate at night, and then with a bed sheet thrown over you. Don't join that kind of operation.

Test a thing to see if it is acceptable to the Lord and don't participate in meaningless and shady activities. Instead, bring them out into the open for the things some people do in secret are so shameful, you can hardly talk about them. Everything that is exposed to the light is clearly visible and that which is clearly visible is obviously on the side of light. That's why it says, "Get up, you sleepyhead, and arise from the dead and God's Son will bathe you in light."

This isn't the admonition to delegates to the convention to get up early for the Bible class. He's saying, "Arise from the dead (that is, from your state of unconscious dreaming) and come into a world of reality." A lot of times people think that Christians are just fuzzy-minded people living in a world of illusion. That isn't true. Those who have gotten up out of their stupor of sin are the ones who are living in the world of reality.

One time about 93 carloads of Ku Klux Klansmen came out to Koinonia and suggested to us that we find a climate a little bit more conducive to our health. We declined it and word got out that I was about to be lynched and some very dear ones came to me and suggested that I find refuge north of the Mason-Dixon line.

I said, "Well, we came here because of the will of God and, if we leave, it will have to be because of the will of God."

They said, "Now, wait a minute here, you been a preacher too long. You get your head out of them theological clouds and face up to reality. That Klan is about to lynch you and you might as well face up to it."

Well, I hadn't been sitting there being shot at and machine-gunned and all like that for three years without being aware of the fact that I was in danger. But I said to them, "Now, what do you mean 'face up to reality'?"

They said, "Be practical. It's all right to discuss theology at the seminary, but you got to face up to the cold stark facts of life."

I said to them, "Now listen, I think I'm the one that's being realistic and you're the one that's being unrealistic. You're facing up to the demands of the Klan which is temporal and transient. And I'm facing up to the demands of God who is eternal. Now who's being realistic? I think God was here before the Klan and I think he'll be here after the Klan is gone. And I think God is more real in this universe than the Ku Klux Klan."

Now Paul is saying here:

Wake up. Get out of your sleep and walk in the reality of daylight. Take extra care, then, how you live. Not like nitwits but like wits. Use your time as though you had to buy it, because there's a lot of wickedness around these days. Therefore, don't be dumb bunnies, but have an intelligent understanding of what the will of the Lord is. Don't get drunk on wine and carry on a lot of foolishness, but tank up on the Spirit. (Now, the word *spirit* here is in the singular.) *But tank up on the Spirit and do your talking to each other with hymns and psalms and spiritual singing and strumming in your hearts to the Lord.* (Might even allow a little bebop hymn occasionally, I don't know.) *Always give thanks for everything to the Father God in the name of our Lord, Jesus Christ.*

From verse twenty-one on to chapter six, verse four, Paul holds a little session in family counseling and he begins it by saying:

You-all put yourselves under one another with Christlike respect. You women, y'all be subject to your men as to the Lord, because a man is head of the woman just as Christ is head of the church and is himself the nerve center of the body. But as the church is subject to Christ, so also women are subject to men in everything.

Now, do you ladies get that? Oh, you say, "He was just a dried-up nubbin of a preacher who never got married. That's the reason he could say that." I don't think that's quite true. I think Paul is showing great insight here. You might not agree that the man is head of the woman, but perhaps it's true right on. It has been my experience in what little bit of marriage counseling I've done that one of the major causes of difficulty in the home is that the husband and wife get confused as to what their role is. Much of the difficulty in the home arises from the fact that the woman wants to be the man and the man is weak enough to let her.

Now Paul is actually drawing an analogy here to the Church and I think what he has to say to the Church, or about the Church, is really more important than what he has to say about marriage. Now when a woman usurps the position of the man, and belittles him and henpecks him and dominates him, all kinds of difficulties arise in the home. So it is with the Church. When the Church, the bride of Christ, becomes dominating and domineering over her husband, which is Christ, all kinds of difficulties arise in the fellowship. The thing that really agitates me is to go into a Sunday school class and hear people sitting around debating whether or not they agree with the Christian teaching, as though the Church wore the britches and they, the Church, were able to dictate to

Jesus Christ, her husband, what he can wear and what he can think and what he can say. If the Church has become increasingly masculine and liberated from the domination of Jesus, the Church has lost something infinitely valuable just as a woman loses something valuable when she refuses to be the object of a man's love.

We see this particularly in the Roman Catholic Church. They have greatly elevated the effeminate side of it, or the Mary side. And I'm quite sure that when these Roman brethren of ours talk about the Virgin Mary, they're talking about the Holy Roman Catholic Church in which she is a symbol and in exalting the Virgin Mary, the woman, they have invariably debased the man. And I think this is why in most Roman Catholic art Jesus is pictured as a weak, effeminate delicate little creature who couldn't by any means compete with the robust health of the Virgin Mary. Now the Church is to let herself be loved and dominated by her husband. And Paul says, this is true of the wife. She must let herself be loved and cared for by her husband.

You men, love your women just as Christ loved the Church and gave himself for her. So that, having bathed her in purity like a bath in water, so to speak, he might stand her by his side, a lovely Church without stain or dirt or anything like that, but that she might be true and pure.

Men, you're supposed to be the head of the household. You're supposed to be the boss. You want to know how? You want to know how to be the boss?

Chrysostom said, "Her that is the partner of thy life, the mother of thy children, the spring of all thy joy, thou must not bind her by terror or threats, but by love and gentleness." You want to know how to be the head of the woman? Love her, like Christ loved the Church. Love her enough to where she knows you're ready to give your life for her. Be head of your woman by being her abject slave. You can rule her that way every time. It really works. She wants to be ruled and dominated by a man who will love her with his very life. Women don't want to dominate the man. They just want a husband that'll love them like a man.

(Men) ought to love their women as though they were their own bodies. He who loves his own woman loves his own body. No one ever hates his own body. But rather, he takes care of it, and grooms it just as Christ does the Church because we are parts of his body.

Here again the sidelight on the Church is tremendously important. When you join that Church, you're joining the most holy, sacred thing in the world. It's not a spiritual Kiwanis Club. It is not set up and founded by human agency. You are coming into a love relationship with your lord, and he does not want this Church of his to become a spiritual prostitute, giving herself to lust and the greed of the people of the world.

For this reason (that is, because of this tremendous self-giving of each other) *a man shall sever his ties to Papa and Mama and shall be wrapped up in his woman, and the two will be a unified body.*

Then Paul, for the first time in any of his writings, admits that he's having a good bit of trouble keeping this analogy going. He says, *Admittedly, this whole thing is quite a puzzle—I mean Christ and the Church.* (He didn't mean about the man and the woman.) Anyway, you-all, every one of you, love your woman as though she were you, and let the woman have respect for her man.

Well, having gotten Mama and Daddy straightened out, he has a word to say to the rest of the family. *"You kids, listen to your parents."* Now he is telling these kids to listen to the kind of parents where the husband loves his wife, just like Christ loved the Church and gave himself for it. And you listen to this Mama who loves her husband and is in subjection to him, and takes care of him. You listen to them, because whenever they say anything they are going to be a unified body.

Respect your father and mother is the first of the ten commandments with a promise attached . . . that it might go well with you and you will live a long time on earth. And you fathers, don't aggravate your kids, but bring them up in the Lord's guidance and counsel.

And then he enters into a little counseling on labor relations:

You workers, co-operate with those over you with humility and respect and with the same kind of loyalty you give to Christ. Not for praise or raise, but as Christ-workers, doing the will of God from your heart. Doing your work with a good attitude as though the Lord, and not men, were your employer.

He says, "When you go to work, don't go to work like a man is employing you. Work at that job as though God himself was employing you." What a high and holy concept of your vocation.

Realize that whether you are a worker or employer, whatever good thing you do will be noticed by the Lord. And you employers, treat your workers the same way. Don't go around breathing down their necks. Understand that both they and you have the same boss, the Lord in heaven, who makes no distinction between employer and employee.

Paul closes with the final personal word: *"Lastly, be strong and courageous men for Christ. Put on God's uniform so as to be able to withstand all the devil's tricks."* Paul wasn't afraid to use pagan terminology to get over a Christian point. *"Put on God's uniform so as to be able to withstand all the devil's tricks. For we're not fighting against ordinary human beings, but against the leaders, politicians and heads of state of this dark world, against spiritual wickedness in high places. Put on God's uniform so you'll be able to put up a fight on the day of battle and, having tended to every detail, make your stand. Therefore, take your position when you have put on the pants of truth, the shirt of righteousness, and the shoes of the good news of peace. Above all, take the bulletproof vest of faith, with which you'll be able to stop the tracer bullets of the evil one. Also, wear the helmet of salvation, and the pistol of the Spirit, which is God's word."*

I want to close with Paul's prayer for the people to whom he was writing and I want it to be my prayer for you:

Peace to the brothers and love mixed with faith from the Father-God and the Lord Jesus Christ. May Divine favor be upon all who unashamedly love our Lord Jesus Christ. Amen.

V

Persisting Threats To Authentic Faith

"You don't take the name of the Lord
in vain with your lips.
You take it in vain with your life."

AN ANCIENT HERESY INCARNATE

The greatest danger to Christianity was not when Jesus was a little babe in Bethlehem with old Herod trying to kill him. That wasn't the most dangerous point in the life of Christianity. I think the most dangerous time was in the second century after Christ, with the rise of the gnostic heresy.

It was a heresy which did not, of course, begin in Christianity; but because it had much in common with Christianity, it sneaked in and almost took it over. It came to its highest apex under the brilliant preaching and teaching of a fellow named Marcion.

Gnosticism comes from the Greek word *gnōsis,* which means "knowledge." *Atheist* means one who does not believe in God. *Agnostic* is one who does not know if there is a God. A *gnostic* is one who claims to have the knowledge. Gnosticism had its roots back in perhaps the fourth century B.C., in the teachings of Plato, and then Aristotle. As Oriental influences came in, this Hellenistic thought mixed with Oriental mysticism, and gnosticism, by the time of Jesus, was just coming into full flower. The heart of gnosticism is dualism—that is, the idea that God is all-good and all-pure and that the earth and all matter is all-evil. The gnostics had worked out this system that God is so good he can't come in contact with the world which is so evil. He could not have created the world; the world is evil and God could not have done it. So they worked out this system of lesser beings. There was a being up there right under God and right under him was one a little lesser than he, etc. Sort of like a military system of the general and the colonel and the major and the captain and the lieutenant and the private first-class and the buck private, and then the guy who has a dishonorable discharge. Now, they couldn't see how this all-pure God could come in contact with this all-evil world, so they said this fallen angel, this guy with the dishonorable discharge, called the "demiurge," was bad enough and still powerful enough to create a wicked world. So their theory of creation was that it was created by the demiurge.

Now, their philosophy of salvation meant that some emanation of the deity had come to earth as God could not come in contact with this earth because it was so evil. They imposed this philosophy upon Christianity. God couldn't really become one with us in this evil old world. So they said that Jesus really did not come in the flesh, he just *seemed* to have flesh. The Greek word for "seem" is *dokeō* and they were called "docetist." They believed Jesus just seemed to be human, but really he wasn't. He couldn't be human because this body is evil and this savior from God couldn't really have a body because it would have been evil for him to have done so.

Salvation meant that you had the right knowledge, the right "gnosis," and could say the right words. Then, when your soul was liberated from this veil of tears and this wicked world, if you could say the right words to the planetary gatekeepers you would be saved. If you had the right scriptures, the right knowledge, then you could be saved.

Now, of course the "Christian" gnostics regarded their doctrines as a superior form of Christianity and themselves alone as the truly spiritual. Logically then, they could not accept the Old Testament at face value with all its history. They had to allegorize it, work it up into schemes of prophecy and all like that. They couldn't deal with a God in history because their God couldn't come in contact with history. So they had to allegorize the Old Testament and find meanings that were not there. Most of the gnostics felt it was easier just to repudiate the Old Testament in full. The concern was no longer with God in history. Rather, history, whether that of the Old Testament or that of Jesus, was sublimated into a dramatic myth, a theological scheme of salvation.

This fellow Marcion was a brilliant preacher of the gnostic philosophy and he certainly had power over the multitudes. He moved to Rome and one of the first things he did was make a big gift to the First Roman Church there. And that, of course, allowed him to speak with authority. He had his name on the brass plate there, and having endowed the Church with money, he now had the authority to be their spiritual guide; and this was the point at which he almost took over the Church. Fortunately, God's Holy Spirit gave the Church wisdom enough to reject Marcion and all his teachings, and Christianity was rescued. But it was not once and for all saved, for Marcion has raised his head time and time again through every century since the birth of Christ. And I think he is walking the streets of this nation of ours daily. He is by no means dead.

When we emphasize the deity of Jesus to the exclusion of the humanity of Jesus, this is pure gnosticism. The gnostics accepted his deity. No question about that. They just denied his humanity. They were quite willing to grant that he was God. In fact, they would ride you out of town if you denied that he was God. They just wouldn't believe that he was flesh, that he had become human.

Now, how do we see this expressed today? I translated the Gos-

pel of Luke and sent it to a denominational magazine and asked
them if they thought it was worthwhile to print a portion of it.
They seized on the chapter in Luke which tells the Christmas story
since they were short on material for their Christmas issue. And
they printed all the Cotton Patch version of the birth of Jesus.
That story tells about the shepherds out on the hillside and the
angels coming and singing "Glory to God in the highest" and they
go into the city and find the baby in a manger. Well now, I was
writing this thing from the cultural standpoint of south Georgia
and there isn't a sheep in the whole southwest part of Georgia; so
how could I have shepherds sitting out in Sumter County when
there weren't any sheep? I couldn't translate that word *shepherds,*
because we didn't have any sheep. There are, however, farmers all
over raising baby chicks, and so I said, "There were some farmers
up late at night with a busted brooder and the glory of the Lord
shown around them. And they said, 'Let's go! Let's go into Gaines-
ville and see what God has done!' "

Well, we haven't had a manger inside Georgia in ten years since
we got rid of all our mules. So I said, "They went and found Joseph and Mary and the baby in an apple box." I was trying to
make that a human situation. I was trying to make Jesus human.
And you know the letters that that poor editor got! They just tore
him up for taking all the dignity out of the Christmas story. There
weren't farmers with a busted brooder! It was shepherds with
sheep. You have broken up our pretty little story by letting Jesus
be a human being! We can't *stand* his incarnation! We want his
deity! The word was God. "Amen, amen!"

If it could be proved beyond any shadow of a doubt that Jesus
Christ of Nazareth was a Negro in the flesh, I know 90 per cent
of the people in the church that excommunicated me would say
Jesus did not come in the flesh. He just seemed to have a body that
was a nigger. We would not accept his humanity if we could prove
beyond a shadow of a doubt that he was not a white man.

I know this to be a truth. A few years ago, just before Christmas,
the father of one of our members at Koinonia was to bring the in-
spirational address at an associational-wide meeting to be held at
a Baptist church in Americus. When his daughter read the announcement in the Americus paper, she said, "Y'all come. Let's
go hear him." Well, at Koinonia, "y'all" means "y'all." It doesn't
mean "you white folks." So, us-all went to that big million-dollar
church. When we went in, they were singing, "Gloria in excelsis
deo." Now, that's gnostic enough not to be earthly—good old Bap-

tists singing Latin. "Glory to God in the highest! On earth, peace, good will to men," and we went in just as they were singing that and we sat down. You know what was the first thing to happen? The folks in front of us moved away. The whole pew vacated. We looked around and the folks back of us had moved away. There we were, a little island in the sanctuary. Nobody in front, nobody behind, an aisle on the left and an aisle on the right.

Shortly, the chairman of the hospitality committee came steaming up the aisle, face flushed. Al Henry was sitting at the end of our pew. The chairman punched Al on the shoulder and said, "He can't stay in here," pointing to the Negro fellow. Al just started singing, "Peace on earth, good will to men." He didn't say anything. The fellow said, "Didn't you hear me? I said, he can't stay in here." Al just kept on singing, "Peace on earth, good will to men." So then the fellow came around this vacant bench which the people had very conveniently vacated for him and stood right in front of the young Negro man, named McGee, and said, "Come on, nigger, you gotta get out of here. You can't stay in here." McGee couldn't sing anything, but he started singing, "Peace on earth, good will to men." I asked him a little later what key he was singing in. He said he didn't know but he thought it was skeleton key —just fit anything, he said. The chairman said, "Didn't you hear me? I said you've got to get out of here. You're disturbing divine worship!" And he was shouting loudly.

Now, I didn't know where the divine worship was, but I did know who was disturbing it. The chairman of the hospitality committee got so infuriated, he lunged over the bench and grabbed McGee and started pulling him over the bench. I moved down, and said, "Now, wait a minute here. Have you got the authority to do this?" I didn't think any church would give the chairman of the hospitality committee that kind of authority. And he said, "Yes, I do." I said, "I'd like to talk with the pastor." He said, "I ain't got time. You got to get out of here." To make a long story short, when they got us outside, the deacons formed a big line and stood between us and the door to the sanctuary to make sure that we couldn't get in again.

The pastor was standing there with them. I turned to him and said, "You know, there's something wrong about tonight, something awfully wrong. On the night when people are singing 'Glory to God in the highest and on earth peace,' for a man to be dragged out of the house of God when his only offense is the color of the skin with which the Almighty endowed him, there's something wrong."

"Yes, I agree," the pastor said, "but this is the policy of our church and I think you all should leave."

I told him, "Well, everything is integrated now except the churches and the jails—and I have hope for the jails."

This fellow Marcion has raised his head time and time again, and I think he is walking the streets of this nation daily. People reject the incarnation by the deification of Jesus. We create in our minds an image of him as a super-being, and thus safely remove him from our present experience and his insistent demands on us. We manage to keep him in this elevated and removed position by not allowing any familiarity with him or the Scriptures. Any attempt to make him human and embarrassingly present is angrily denounced as sacrilegious. By carefully preserving our image of him as God, we no longer have to deal with him as the Son of Man. Preachers by the dozens who vehemently affirm his deity shamelessly deny his humanity if he is black and poor.

JUDAS

This man that I want to talk to you about is a man whom I perhaps feel more love for, more compassion for, than any other man in the whole Bible. Somehow I feel more akin to him than any other man and if I call him the man whom Jesus loved it might be that I'm reading a little bit of my own personal feelings in it because I'm so kin to him that I want to feel like the man whom Jesus loved. We think of John as being "the beloved disciple." Everywhere we find books talking about John, the beloved disciple. But you know I read through the Gospels trying to find out the basis for John being the beloved disciple. I found that Matthew didn't call John the beloved disciple. I found that Mark didn't call John the beloved disciple. I found that Luke didn't call John the beloved disciple. The only place I found it was in the Gospel of John. Now that made me a little bit leery of this man's opinion of himself and I began to search and I found that John *wanted to be* the beloved disciple. He *wanted to be* with all he had. Now, I think Jesus did love John, but not to the extent that John thought he did. I think the real beloved disciple was Judas Iscariot. Because Judas got the major share of Jesus' love, John was terribly jealous of him. And when you begin to find some theories to account for Judas' betrayal of his Lord, John's theory always is that it was because he was a devil from the beginning. (*That old devil got the place that I want. He got ahead of me.*) So John's Gospel was written partly out of jealousy, I think, of Judas, and his explanation of Judas' being a devil from the beginning must not be taken too seriously. On the last night Jesus said, "One of you is going to betray me." They all began looking around at one another and said, "Who is it? Is it I? Is it I?" And nobody had any real clue. Now if this man had been a devil from the beginning, why didn't John at least have some inkling of it at the close of the ministry of Christ?

No, Judas was not a devil from the beginning. John tries to leave us with the impresion that Judas betrayed Jesus because he loved money. John tells about the lady that came in with the precious perfume and broke it on Jesus' feet, and how Judas said it should be sold and given to the poor. John said Judas really didn't care anything about the poor, he just wanted the money to go into the treasury so he could steal it. Well now, if John knew all that embezzlement was going on, why didn't he call for the election of a new treasurer? I mean, there's something wrong about a man's interpretation of his brother when he reads back into it his own jealousy and his own feelings.

So then we raise the question, "What is the position of this man?" What was the pressure put on him that caused him to betray the man he loved? There is a theory that Judas was a little bit impatient with Jesus up there at Galilee. Preaching at all those civic clubs, and kissing a few babies and all, wasn't really getting the movement *going.* He wanted to put the heat on Jesus to expose him, to tell him to get going, to set this movement on the wing. This theory pictures Judas as a Zealot. But I do not think Jesus would have wanted to have two Zealots in his group. These Zealots were the superduper patriots of the day. And while Jesus could contain one, I seriously doubt that he could have contained two. And since Simon the Zealot was in his group, I don't think Judas was a Zealot by any means.

What, then, was the pressure? What caused his reaction? Now, we have very scarce material to draw this man's picture. We don't have a whole lot told to us, and to use some of it we have to kind of project through imagination. This isn't entirely unscientific. In the Smithsonian Institution, you go up into the dinosaur room and they've got big skeletons of dinosaurs, forty-fifty feet long. Now, they haven't found that many dinosaur bones lying around. They've found one or two, maybe a tibia, and from that they measure and make projections and make this whole big dinosaur out of the projections from one or two bones. Now if the scientist can make a dinosaur out of a tibia, there's nothing wrong with reconstructing Judas out of two or three passages from the Scriptures, with a little bit of imagination to go along with it. I'm going to put a good bit of plaster in here and there, but there'll always be some solid bones from which to project our thought.

Jesus chose his group almost entirely from Galilee. He himself was called the Galilean and most of those who were with him were Galileans. But Jesus chose one from Judea. In fact, I think in the choosing of his twelve he was trying to get a fair sampling of society. I think great thought went into the choosing of the twelve. He wanted a little microcosm of Judaism. He had Matthew the Publican and Simon the Zealot. I never would have chosen either one of them had I been in Jesus' position. But they were part of the fabric of society and he had to choose them. It was as though he was getting a cross-section of all society and so he had to choose at least one who represented the hard and orthodox, or fundamentalist, viewpoint. Now, coming from Judea, Judas was a man from the stronghold of orthodoxy. He was from the South. This was the Bible belt in Palestine. Down there everybody quoted the Scriptures and toted the Bible. This is where the denominational headquarters were—the printing press, everything. When they established the synagogue, it was a Southern Bapt—it was a Southern synagogue. God didn't just make an annual swing there during the August revival, he *lived* there! That was God's dwelling place on Mt. Zion. And this is where man had to go to worship him.

Now, if ever a man was an orthodox, Bible-toting, Scripture-quotin' man, Judas was. I think that coming from this fervent religious background he was saturated with the Old Testament scriptures. I imagine he saturated himself in the social problems and he loved Micah, Josea, Isaiah, Amos. Oh, he loved to read those men. How he longed for the day when the real warmth of the fire of the prophets would break loose in Judaism and take the place of the cold, liturgical, meaningless new moons and sabbaths and sacrifices. I think Judas must have been a man of great social passion. And when the woman broke that bottle of perfume Judas was really, honestly, concerned about the poor. It wasn't that he wanted to steal the money. He wanted to feed the poor. And he thought it a tragic waste for the perfume to be wasted when there are so many poor people. That's a legitimate objection, I think. More than likely this man was the chairman of the Social Action Committee of the twelve. His concern was for the poor even on that last night, and when he dipped in the dish with Jesus and Jesus said, "What thou doest, do quickly," all the apostles thought he meant for Judas to go out and buy some bread for the poor. Judas had been in the habit of doing that. And he would collect clothing. He would be in charge of the Thanksgiving basket. He would be in charge of all of the work of trying to help the poor because he had immersed himself in the social problems. So that when Jesus came into Judea preaching, "The spirit of the Lord is upon me; he hath anointed me to preach the Gospel to the poor," I imagine Judas really responded to that. Here's a man who had the warmth, the vitality, the great compassion, the fire of the prophets.

And Jesus looked at Judas and saw in him a really consecrated, dedicated young man. Judas fell in love with Jesus, and Jesus fell in love with Judas. There was no mockery of calling Judas and saying, "Well, you know, I got to have me a devil. Judas, would you like to be the devil for me? I got to have somebody to betray me." Certainly not this. This does violence to our Master. I think he chose Judas in all sincerity just as he called Peter or John or Andrew or any of the others and he called them because he loved them and because he wanted them as part of the fellowship. I think Judas responded because he honestly saw in Jesus the fulfillment of his hopes for social justice and righteousness in his own day.

So then, following the Galilean campaign, came the heavy days of preaching, when Jesus would send them out, and he'd send Judas along with them and they would cast out devils. They would preach the Gospel. The poor would have the Good News proclaimed to them. There was a time of instruction when Jesus gathered them about him and taught them the great Lesson on the Mount. I would not be at all surprised but that Judas learned that before any of them did. And I think they all had to memorize it. It was a whole body of thought that Jesus had put together and made every last one of those disciples memorize it from top to bottom. Judas learned it. He was a good disciple and a good Jew. I think he was happy with Jesus, greatly devoted to him, willing to perform any task, menial as it might be, fulfilling the task of handling the money—about the hardest job that a man could possibly have.

Now I've got to really use a little plaster. The twelve moved on into Judea and Jesus set his pace to go to Jerusalem, to go into the very face of the orthodoxy which can quote Scripture and slit a man's throat at the same time, the orthodoxy which can quote the prophets and engineer a crucifixion. Jesus knew this schizophrenia of orthodoxy and he set his face to go into the midst of it

and I imagine that it was with great fear and trembling that Judas
followed him into Jerusalem. He wanted to stay up North where
everybody'd gone liberal. He didn't want to go back into that
stronghold of orthodoxy. But Jesus felt that's where he had to go
and that's where he went. Jesus had gone out and got himself a
mule. He told them, "I want you to go get me a son of an ass"
(that's the south Georgia way of saying get me a mule) and he
says, "I want one whereon no man has ever sat." Now, if you think
Jesus was an effeminate man, you just try to ride a mule whereon
no man has sat! I tried that once! And when I got through he *still*
was a mule whereon no man had sat! It's bad enough to ride a mule
like that on the back forty, but to ride down the main street of
Jerusalem you got to be really a horseman. Our Lord must've
really been a man among men to ride that mule with all that com-
motion going on. The authorities came out and tried to tell him
to shut up and stop parading without a permit, saying "You got
to quit this. Tell them to shut up. Tell them to quit all this demonstration." And Jesus said, "Listen, boys, you're behind the
times. If I tell my disciples to shut up, the very rocks will cry out!"
He's saying, man, this movement's gone too far, I can't stop it by
trying to squelch a few people here. All nature's been caught up
into this movement. It's on the move. And if these people hush,
the rocks will take up the song of freedom and first thing you
know the Confederate monument in the square will start singing
"We Shall Overcome." You can't stop this thing, he's saying.

When they couldn't stop him by bringing charges of parading
without a permit, the authorities get real worried, and the man
that worried most was the chief high priest named Caiaphas. I
imagine old Caiaphas up in the third story of the Temple in his
private study looking out his window and watching that big
crowd. He had but forty-two at his preaching service Sunday
morning. Here comes Jesus with several thousand. Now that kind
of statistics never promotes fraternal relationships. Caiaphas begins to get real worried about a man who has such power over the
masses. He can't understand how a fellow like Martin Luth— I
mean Jesus, could get so many people to be loyal to him, when he
couldn't even get a deacon's meeting going.

So Caiaphas begins to watch and he sees a man he recognizes.
He gets his binoculars and looks—yeah! There's that guy—Judas
Iscariot. I knew him. He was a student at the seminary when I
used to work up there in the North. He was a good boy. I think
I'm going to get him up here. That night Judas has a special
courier from the pope— from the high priest, who brought him a

message saying, "His Excellency would like to see you in his study tonight at 9 P.M." Well, to be invited for a private interview with the pope is quite an honor and so Judas decides to go and he walks in and is greeted warmly by the high priest:

"Glad to see you. You're a good boy, Judas. I've known you ever since you were a little bitsy tyke. I remember you in my Sunday school when I was pastor of your chur— your synagogue out there. You got a good mama and a good daddy. Bless their heart, I know they brought you up right. They hadn't handed you any of this wild agitation stuff. You're a good boy. You know, I remember how bright you were. You used to be my altar boy. I remember the way you read the Scriptures. You had such promise. I don't know what happened to you, but here you've kind of strayed. Now Judas, wouldn't you like to come back in? You know, I happen to have a report on this synagogue over there at Capernaum—they're without a rabbi over there. I think we could fix you up with a real good position if you'd go on and get a little bit more schooling and quit this business. Furthermore, this guy you're running around with, this little Galilean peasant that's got all these folks singing and shouting and clapping their feet, carrying on all that irreligious truck they're doing in the street down there. You know, he's not much of a guy to get all the folks out in the street like that. You might be interested in a little information I have about him. I've been keeping a file on him, Judas." Maybe he goes over to his steel drawer and pulls out a big manila folder and says, "Now look here, I got a report here from the un-Roman Activities Committee. They have found out that—I hate to say this, Judas—but they report there's pretty good evidence that he's a Communist. It is reported that he practices with his group the common purse. Do you know anything about that, Judas?" "Well, yes, I've heard something about that." "You know, Judas, the RBI is gonna come down here and arrest him—there isn't any question about it. And they're going to arrest all these other guys who are with him. Now I'd hate to see a good boy like you ruined. You got such a good record and such a good future, it'd be such a shame to have a good boy like you ruined by associating with this young man here."

Perhaps Judas says, "But, sir, he speaks as no man ever spoke. He interprets the Word of God."

"Judas, he can't interpret the Word of God. He didn't graduate from our seminary. You know that. Now listen, get that out of your head. He's a heretic!! He's no man of God. Why look at him. I had some men watching him and he even breaks the Ten Commandments. He goes against Moses. And more than that he says they're going to tear down this place, not leaving one stone upon another —gonna destroy the Temple and this holy place. He breaks the Sabbath. He transgresses the law. He's not even a man of God. You run around with a fella like that?"

"Oh, but, sir, he preaches the word, his love, to look in his eyes . . . his compassion. Come out, I beg you, sir. Come to just one meeting when he preaches. I want you to just hear him."

"Judas, you're asking *me* to come hear that guy preach? No, no. Now get straight, I don't want to argue with you."

Judas leaves, shaken, his heart pounding. Here the highest ecclesiastical authority is putting the pressure on him. He's also feeling the tremendous tug and pull of the Lord. Here's a man torn— split—not neutral. This man is not guilty of the sin of neutrality. He loves Caiaphas. He loves the organized framework of Judaism —the pageantry. Its beauty, its psalms, incense—all these things are wonderful. And he does not hate it. But he wants to see it filled with meaning, with life. Here he is caught between the two.

I can imagine him going out and saying to Jesus, "Master, don't you think there's something really good about Judaism? Why do you call the religious leaders 'whitewashed sepulchers'? There are other names you could call them like 'you good white people.' That would be nice. And it would be politics. Don't infuriate people needlessly. Why trample on toes when you don't have to trample on toes? Why do you call 'em all kinds of names and say they are like 'graves which appear not as men walk over unaware'? Why do you call them blind Pharisees? Be a little more gentle with them."

Perhaps Jesus is saying to him: "You can't put new wine in old skins. If you do, you'll lose your wine and ruin your skin. You don't put a new patch on an old garment. If you do, it'll split the patch and destroy the garment. You can't do that."

"Oh, but, sir, we could go a bit slower, couldn't we? I mean, really now, this business has been here a long time and it is going to take a long time to get over it. Couldn't you go just a wee bit slower?"

"No man who has set his hand to the plow and then looks back is worthy of the kingdom of God. . . . He that loves mother or father, brother or sister more than me cannot be my disciple. . . . Except a man take up his cross and follow me, he cannot be my disciple . . ."

Here are two diametrically opposed forces, with Judas caught in the midst of the two. Now, I must read you a little to show you what's going on at this time in the mind of the Master.

Then Jesus comes with them into a field which is called Geth-semane. And says to his students, "Sit here while I go over yonder and pray." And he took with him Rock and the two Zebedee boys and he began to be gravely agitated and emotionally stirred up. Then he says to them, "My soul is grieved . . ., my soul is exceedingly grieved. Stay here and be on the alert with me." And he went a little further and he fell on his face and he prayed and he said, "Oh, my father, if it is at all possible, let this cup pass from me. But yet I don't want it as I wish it, but as you will it." Then he comes to his disciples and he finds them sleeping and he says to Rock, "So you were not able to stay on the alert and pray with me? You be on your tiptoes and pray that you do not enter into temptation." Again the second time he goes and prays and says, "Oh, my father, if it be possible, let this cup pass from. . . . If this cup cannot pass from me except I drink it, let your will be done." And he comes again and he found them asleep . . . he came again and found them asleep for their eyes were weighted down and he left them and went again and prayed the third time, saying the same thing, and again he comes to them . . . to the disciples, and he says to them, "All right, sleep on a little while now and refresh your-selves." Then a little while later he says, "Listen! The hour has come. The son of man is turned over into the hands of sinners. You all get up! Let's go! The man who is going to turn me in is here."

Now, we think this Agony in the Garden of Gethsemane is the agony of Jesus' approaching crucifixion. I don't see that at all in this. Not one time is the cross mentioned. The cup, the terrible cup that he's talking about here is not the cup of crucifixion. It's the cup of betrayal. It's the cup of having a man that he has lav-ishly loved, a man whom he has called and fixed his hopes upon, having that man torn asunder and tormented by this terrible ten-sion. It's *that* cup that Christ is referring to here. Does it not seem reasonable that he who came to die for sinners would, on his last night on earth, be most concerned about a sinner? Would it seem natural that Our Lord on his last night would be most concerned about himself when he came to give his life as ransom for many? Does it not seem more reasonable that his last agonizing concern would be for this man who was at that moment most severely tempted? And he was saying to his other disciples, "I've been pray-ing for this boy of mine—you-all pray that you not be tempted. . . ."

Like who? Like Judas at this very moment. He was asking them to be on the alert with him. Now here comes Judas and this is where we get some real insights into the heart of the Master as we watch him in his dealings with Judas:

*And while he was speaking to them, behold Judas, one of the twelve, came and with him a whole big crowd of priests and elders of the people of Jerusalem, with swords and clubs and the one who betrayed him gave them a sign saying, "He whom I kiss, this is He . . . and you seize him." And right away he came up to Jesus and he said*s *"Rabbi, hello, Rabbi." And he kissed him and he kissed him and he kissed him.* Thayer defines this word as meaning "to kiss much, to kiss with deep emotion." The Greeks had two words for "kiss." They had three words for "love." These fellows really wanted to be precise in these relationships. And one of these words they had for "kiss" is rather unemotional. It's a greeting kind of thing, almost the equivalent of a handshake. It's the kind of kiss you give your wife when you're rushing off to catch a bus. There's not much of it.

Now I imagine Caiaphas had called Judas in the second time:

"I saw you with that guy again and next time I see you, Judas, I'm gonna turn you out of the First Synagogue of Jerusalem. I'm not going to have you going around with this heretic."

Excommunication for a Jew was death—economically, socially, and every way. And it was at this point, I think, that Judas finally capitulated and said, "Oh, no, sir, don't do that."

"All right, Judas, this man's gonna get arrested . . . he's gonna get the whole nation into trouble. It's much better that one man be salted away than to get the whole nation into trouble. I'll put him away. I'll put him in the jail until all this demonstration and all this civil rights movement and everything dies down . . . and then I can get him out again and everything will be all right."

So Judas gives in and says, "All right, yes . . . yes . . . yes. I'll show you who he is."

Perhaps Caiaphas says, "Now you know it's much better to get him at night than in daytime because of all these demonstrations going on. You know a lot of other folks are around him—all of them growing beards and everything. If we go out there at night to try to get him we're liable to get the wrong one. We don't want to get the wrong possum in the trap. Now, Judas, is there some way that you could point him out to us?"

Perhaps it is at this moment that Judas says, "Why, yes. It's the one whom I kiss (and he uses the unemotional word) . I'll just run up to him right quick (indicates a peck on the face) like that and you grab him quick. That'll be the one."

But when Judas gets there in the garden, he goes up and says, "Hello . . . hello, Rabbi. Hello." And he goes up to Jesus and puts his arm around him and starts to give him the little quick kiss and he can't! His arms freeze around the neck of his Lord. He can't tear them loose. And he suddenly uses his other word for "kiss," which doesn't appear very often in the Scriptures. It's used only in times of great emotion. It is the kind of kiss you give a man who is closer to you than your own heart. Judas thought it'd be a peck on the cheek. But his arms froze around his Master's head and he kissed him . . . and he kissed him . . . and he kissed him. And then Jesus says something very significant. It's translated, "Friend, why are you here?" But the word in the Greek—again they have various words. One word for "friend" comes from this unemotional word for "kiss." It means a friend in the rather abstract. But there was another Greek word for "friend" that is real close. When you use it in the feminine sense it means a girl-friend—one with whom you are deeply in love. When you use it in the masculine sense it's about the equivalent of the word "buddy." And Jesus, when Judas is there hugging him and kissing him and crying, says to Judas, "Oh, my buddy, my buddy. Has it come to this? I've just been praying hours through the night for you, old boy. I know the torment of your soul. I know the pressure that this Caiaphas can put on a man. I know the pressure of childhood rearing, and tradition. I know, Judas, and I've been praying . . . I've been praying—oh, God, I've been praying—that you could come through it. Has it come to this, my buddy? My buddy." Now this was not sarcasm. This was no "Friend, why are you here?" spoken in nasty voice. Here were two men who deeply, sincerely, and honestly loved one another.

But what will happen now? Judas is a man without a high priest. His professional high priest, Caiaphas, has jilted him. He has betrayed his prophetic high priest, his Lord. He's a man with no contact with God. What's he going to do? He'd go back as far as he could to make amends. He goes back to Caiaphas. Takes the little old gift that Caiaphas had given him, the little old thirty pieces of silver that had happened to be jangling in Caiaphas' pocket at the time. He goes back and he finds the high priest and he flings the money down and he says, *"Take your rotten money. I have betrayed innocent blood. I should never have let you put me up to this!"* And he says, "Take it back!" And old Caiaphas mockingly says, "Well, you see we got our man."

Judas goes out into the night, jilted by his profesional priest . . . having betrayed his prophetic priest—a man with no approach to God and he looks for a rope and he finds one. He goes out and finds a tree and he climbs it and jumps off. Luke says that when he did this his body burst asunder so that his bowels gushed out. Now, the Hebrews, as well as the Greeks, thought of the bowels as being the seat of the emotions, the home of the soul. It's like saying that all of Judas' motions burst out, burst asunder. I don't want to read too much into this, but I wonder if in this last agonizing moment Judas' body didn't symbolize his soul. Just as his body was the victim of the tension of two opposing forces—the upward pull of the rope and the downward pull of gravity—so it seems to me that this man's soul had been the victim of two opposing forces—the cold, priestly, professional ecclesiasticism of his day, gone to seed, still maintaining the fires on an altar to a God whom they had forgotten, and this Lord whom he loved better than life itself.

This is not the tragedy of a neutral man. This is the tragedy of a man who tried to take two sides. And the result was the same as it always is: death for him, and death for the man he loved.

TAKING THE NAME IN VAIN

Thou shalt not take the name of the Lord thy God in vain, for the Lord will not hold him guiltless that taketh his name in vain.

What is this "taking the name of the Lord"? Well, early in the biblical writings we find that the Hebrews were not content to call themselves by the name of their nation. They were a nomadic tribe, they were wandering around. They didn't stay still long enough, really, to be called Canaanites or Egyptians or Assyrians. They were on the go, so they took the name of their deity. This is familiar to us. We take the name of our deities, our founders. Mohammedans take the name of Mohammed, Buddhists take the name of the Buddha, Christians take the name of the Christ—we are familiar with taking the name.

We have gotten off the track, though, when we speak of "taking the name in vain." We have somehow come to believe that it means to get out on the street corner and use God's name in a vulgar way. But you cannot take a name in vain if you have never taken it to begin with. I can get out here on the street corner and say "Buddha damn" all day long and never take the name of Buddha in vain. I have never taken the name of Buddha. I haven't circulated it around that I am a disciple of Buddha. I cannot take his name in vain. First I have to take it.

Now the words *in vain* mean "empty and meaningless, of no account, of no seriousness." We take it and on we go and it means nothing. We keep sailing under the same old banner, living the same old life, having the same old attitudes, walking in the same old way. The name has meant nothing to us. It doesn't change us. You don't take the name of the Lord in vain with your lips. You take it in vain with your life. It isn't the people outside the church who take God's name in vain. They've never taken it so they can't take it in vain. It's the people on the inside, the nice people who would not dare let one little cuss word fall over their lips—they're the ones many times whose lives are totally unchanged by the grace of God. They're the ones who take the name in vain.

What makes us different? "You-all be different because I am different," Jesus said. What is it that distinguishes you? The Christians got the idea that when God gave you a name he had made you his son, he had adopted you into his family, and from that time on you were flying under his banner and under his name and that you would tremble in your boots if you let that name be anything less than holy, And this is what Jesus is trying to say to us when he said to pray, "Hallowed be thy name—let your name mean something."

God is interested in his name. He's interested in it because the only way he has of making himself known to mankind is through the people who bear his name. You can see him in the lightning and hear him in the thunder; you can watch the mighty waves roll. But God cannot really make himself known to mankind unless he has some flesh—human flesh—through which to make himself known. If God ever comes to our churches, it'll be because he comes riding in on our hearts, not banging in the door and sitting there in the temple waiting for us to get there. We bear his name and this is the only way he has of making himself known to the people.

In other words, the word *God* is a rather undefined word for most people. We have to experience it. And I think others who know him and who bear the name translate it for us not through the way they talk nor through the way they pray nor even through the way they preach, but through the way they live. If we see something different in them, if we see something holy in them, then they are communicating to us and they are defining in a very real sense the meaning of the word *God* to us.

Now, Jesus in his last night on earth really prayed what is the "Lord's Prayer." This was his prayer. I want you to notice how concerned he was about this "name":

Jesus spoke these things and lifted up his eyes into the sky and said, "O Father, the hour has arrived; validate your Son, that the Son might validate you, just as you have given to him authority over all flesh that everyone whom you have given to him, he might give to them spiritual life. This is the spiritual life, that they may know the only true God and the one whom you've sent, Jesus Christ. I have validated you upon the earth, and I have completed the work which you gave me to do. And now, validate me, Father, with the credentials which I had with you before the world was. I have clearly revealed your name to the men whom you gave to me out of the world; they are mine and you gave them to me and they have kept your word. Now they have known that all things which you have given to me are from you; and the words which you have given to me I have turned over to them and they have caught on and they know, truly, that I have come from you; and they have caught on to the fact that you have sent me. I pray for them; I'm not now praying for the world, but for these which you have given to me because they are mine; and everything that's mine is yours and everything that's yours is mine, and I am glorified in them. Now, I am no longer in the world, and yet they are in the world, and I am coming to you. O Holy Father, keep them in the name which you have given to me that they might be one even as we are one."

He's praying that they might be kept "in the name." The only way the world can ever come to have spiritual life is to see this life bursting in and out of them and being translated into flesh, thus continuing the incarnation over and over again, so that Jesus now has not just one body, but hundreds of fragments scattered throughout the world all bearing the same name. When the world sees these people, it sees in them such characteristics as being peacemakers. Men say, "Ah, there is a son of God." Why? Because they see in this man the image, the characteristics of the Father.

I was out hunting one time when I was home from college and I got lost way back in the woods. I finally came to a little clearing and there was an old farmer sitting on his porch chewing tobacco. I didn't know who he was, but I went up to him and I asked him how could I get to such and such a road. He sat there chewing and looking at me with piercing eyes. He didn't answer my question. He looked at me and said, "I know who you are."

I said, "Well, I don't think so, sir. I have never been in these parts before. I'm lost. I don't think you've ever seen me."

"Yes, I know who you are. You're Jim Jordan's boy, ain't ya?"

I said, "Yes, sir. That's right. How'd you know?"

"Well," he said, "You're just the spitting image of him."

He had seen in me the image of my father. I didn't put a name on my forehead, I didn't tell him my name; he said, "image." That identified me.

I think when people see people of peace, of reconciliation, of mercy, of humility, of kindness, they look upon these and say, "I know who you are. I've seen the image of the Father. You're God's boy."

As the world looks at us today, how do we define the name? What do men associate with God as they would look upon our own lives, our life together in the church community? What is it which distinguishes us? What sets us apart? What makes us different is that we are flying under a different banner, living a different life, committed to a different set of values? Are we distinguishable people today? If not, it could be that the name is meaning little or nothing to us. It could be we are taking the name in vain. Now, to do this is a very, very serious offense. It is the "unpardonable sin." "Thou shalt not take the name of the Lord thy God in vain." Why? "For the Lord will not hold him guiltless that taketh his name in vain." "Will not hold him guiltless" is a rather round-about way of saying he will hold him guilty—that is, he will not pardon him. Taking the name of the Lord in vain is the unpardonable sin.

"Taking the name in vain" is playing the hypocrite, it's flying under false banners. The word *hypocrite* is a rather interesting one. Our English word is just a transliteration of the Greek word, *hypokritēs*. It's a word that comes from the Greek theater. It means a play-actor. In those days, actors played many different parts. A man would run off the stage and get a mask, come back on and play a part, run off the stage and get another mask, and come back on and play another part. He could play a half dozen or more parts in one Greek drama by the use of masks. These people were called *hypokritēs,* "play-actors." Now, originally, they did it legitimately. That was their business—to play a role, to play a part. But the word *hypo* means "under," *kritēs* means "to judge" or "to evaluate." It means one who must be judged, ultimately and evaluated by that which is under, not by that which is on the outside.

A hypocrite, then, is one whose character ultimately is determined not by what men see on the outside, but what God finds on the inside. Those two things don't always coincide. This is what makes taking the name of the Lord such a dangerous kind of thing. Do we find this in the New Testament? Yes.

Look at Luke, the twelfth chapter:

Now, when the great crowds had gathered together so that they stepped on one another's toes, he began to say to his students, "First of all, above everything else I have to tell you, chiefest of everything, you keep your eye peeled for the leaven of the Pharisees, which is play-acting."

Chiefest of everything I've got to warn you against, of all the sins—adultery, murder, stealing—chiefest of all is play-acting. Then he goes on to define it at great length.

There's nothing veiled which shall not be unveiled and there is nothing secret which shall not be brought out into the open. And whatever you speak in the darkness shall be heard in the light, and whatever you whisper in the ears in your bedrooms shall be broadcast from the rooftops. I want to tell you, my friends, don't you be scared of those who kill the body and then have nothing more that they can do to you. Don't you be scared of those.

He says, "Your physical life is not the vantage point from which to make your deepest decisions." I think part of what he means by "eternal life" is that you view life from the vantage point of eternity, not from the little tiny time-space span that you happen to be occupying at that particular moment. Your vision is of eternity; it's a life lived in the light of eternity rather than in the light of the immediate present. "So," he said, "Don't you be scared of those who kill the body and then have nothing further they can do."

But I would point my finger at him whom you shall fear: you be afraid of him who, when he has killed, has the power to throw you into "Gehenna." I want to tell you something. You be scared of him.

Now, who is Jesus talking about? Don't be afraid of an assassin; he's really a little nincompoop. Isn't much he can do but blow your brains out. But there is somebody you better be afraid of— it's the guy who can throw you into hell. Who is it? It's this play-actor; he plays the role of being a leader, a leader of the blind, and he says, "Come on and follow me, I'll lead you into the light," and he is blind. The blind leading the blind—they both fall into the pit of Gehenna. It's the man who says, "I know God, I can lead you to God." And you fall in behind him and find that he's playing a role. He's a wolf in sheep's clothing, and you trust your soul to him and he leads you into the pit. You had better keep your eye on him.

Also, we had better exercise some moral judgment. Don't let this business of "judge not" throw you. Jesus didn't say, "Judge not." He said, "Don't you set yourself up as a judge with the idea that you yourself will escape judgment." He said, "By their fruits you shall know them. Judge their fruits." Now, he might not have made us a judge, but he made us a fruit inspector. We better inspect the fruits. Before you put your soul in the hands of a man, you had better find out whether he's playing a role or whether he's the real stuff. Lift up that sheepskin, even if it does have D.D. written on it and look underneath it. You'll know them not by the inscriptions, but by the way they live.

Why is this "play-acting" the unpardonable sin? You can read the New Testament through and not once do you find Jesus saying to a hypocrite, "Thy sins be forgiven." He said it to a harlot, he said it to a tax gatherer, he said it to all kinds of people. But he never said it to a hypocrite. He couldn't.

Let's look at an example which Jesus gave. He said two men went up into the temple to pray. One was a Pharisee, and he was a nice Pharisee. He would've qualified as chairman of the board of deacons in any of our churches. He prayed. He was there for midweek prayer meetings every time, which is certainly something. He was a tither, and that's not to be sneered at. And he was a "faster." That meant he really observed all the religious observances. He was there for Easter, he was there for every holiday and every holy day. He was there for the pastor's anniversary; he contributed quite a bit to the fund for the purchase of the new automobile. He was an active member of the religious establishment. In fact, he was so proud of his record that he was afraid God had lost it. And so he proceeds to reopen the file so that if God, perchance, had lost the original, he could furnish him with a carbon. And he begins to inform God of just what his qualifications are; and they are considerable. On the other hand, there was this old Publican. These were people who were about the equivalent of a fellow traveler. They collaborated with the military occupying forces to collect the taxes from the Jewish people; and they were about the most despised and unpopular people. You couldn't have held up a more despicable person than Jesus did. He lets this man, the lowest man on the totem pole, go to the same temple. Now, he didn't ask God to open his file; he had to begin with just a very simple prayer: "O God, have mercy on me, the sinner."

Now, Jesus raises the question, which of them got his prayers answered? They both did; they both got their prayers answered. The old publican asked for forgiveness and that's what he got. The old Pharisee asked for nothing and that's what he got. Read it. He asked for nothing whatsoever. His was one of these informative prayers. He just told God what was going on.

There was an old deacon down in that little church I grew up in. Every Sunday morning, he would read the Atlanta *Journal* in the King James English. "Lord, thou knowest this," and "Lord, thou knowest that," and "Lord, thou knowest what's happened over here," and "Lord, thou knowest what's happened over there"; and then, he would pick up the town gossip and inform the Lord of all that. Well, I admit the Lord, getting up rather late on Sunday morning, may have appreciated a briefing on the part of this deacon; but I should think that God can handle the news quite well himself.

The hypocrite, generally, is unpardonable because this is the one condition of the soul in which a man dares not ask for forgiveness. It's unpardonable simply because no pardon is asked, no pardon is requested. God won't grant a prayer that isn't uttered. He can stand at the door and knock; but he can't shoot the lock off. He can only come in to the extent that we invite him in and ask him in. Why do we not ask for a pardon? Well, Jesus goes on in this same passage, in the twelfth chapter of Luke:

Are not five sparrows sold for two bits? And not one of them is unremembered by God. Moreover, even the hairs on your head are all numbered. So quit being afraid.

He said, you're dealing with a God of detail, a God who is quite aware of even little five-for-a-quarter birds and he's quite aware of even the hairs on our heads. So, he said, since God is a God of great detail, you really need not be afraid. You can trust yourself to him.

Now, I want to tell you something, that everyone who confesses me before mankind, I'll stand up with him before men. Now, whoever denies me before mankind, then he shall be denied before the angels of God. (The denial here really means "to take the name in vain". Oh sure, he's got my name, but he's denying with his life that he has any partnership with me.) *Now, everyone who speaks a word against the son of Man, it shall be forgiven him. But he who blasphemes the Holy Spirit, it shall not be forgiven him.*

Blaspheming the Holy Spirit is the unpardonable sin. And that, too, is hypocrisy. He's still talking here about hypocrisy. This word *blaspheme,* again, is a transliteration of the Greek. We English people speak an awful lot of unconscious Greek. It's just brought over into the English. The word is from the Greek *blasphēmeō*. This is a compound word: *blas*—and I almost hesitate to translate that word. It's a case of onomatopoeia—it is what it sounds like. It means "to pass gas," to create a stink, literally. The word *phēmeō* —our English word *fame* comes from that—means "to circulate the fame or report." Then *blasphēmeō* means "to circulate a stinking report." That's literally what it means.

Now, how do you circulate a stinking report? Well, you say, "Look, the Holy Spirit lives in me" and inside you're full of dead-men's bones, you stink to high heaven. This is what Jesus jumped on the Pharisees about. He said, "Oh, sure, outside you're white-washed sepulchers. But inside you stink to high heaven." When you say the Holy Spirit lives in that kind of filth, you're circulating a stinking report about the Holy Spirit.

The Holy Spirit is concerned about his name, and he has turned over his name to us. He's given me his name; and I've got a responsibility to bear that name, to bear it in honesty and sincerity. What, then, makes this blasphemy unpardonable? Is it unpardonable from God's side? No. There is no unpardonable sin from God's side. If we confess our sin, he is faithful and just and forgives us our sin. On God's side, there is no such thing as an unpardonable sin, be it murder, adultery—anything. There is nothing on God's side that's unpardonable. Well, then, why should it not be forgiven? Simply because we will not confess our sin. This is what the hypocrite will not do. The play-actor is concerned about *covering* his sin and not about *confessing* it.

Suppose that I were a highly respected pastor of a church. My people had great confidence in me and I sought and cultivated that confidence. But suppose on the side I lived a life of my own doing; and when my church thought that I was off at a minister's school, I was off with lady friends. But I kept this quite apart from my ministerial life. No one knew about it. But suppose some of my lady friends had a venereal disease. And I contracted syphilis. I'm aware that today medical science can cure syphilis. It's not an incurable disease any more. It is curable. But it's curable under the condition that it's detectable. I realize that I've got it. Now what can I do? There stands medical science ready, anxious, willing, capable, and able to cure it. But I've got to go to a doctor and somebody's got to be in on my secret. In other words, I've got to cut a little hole in my mask for someone to peer through. Now, I know that it might become community news and with it will go all this confidence that I have so carefully built up. All of my future, my hopes, my aspirations are sailing on this, on my ability to keep out one little tiny ray of inspection. So, on one little blister after another, I put a Band-Aid; and my syphilis goes uncured, not because medical science is unwilling to cure it, but because I am unwilling to confess it.

Hypocrisy, play-acting, is the one condition of the soul in which man asks for no forgiveness, for to do so makes him have to confess that he's a sinner. At the moment he confesses that he's a sinner, he's no longer a play-actor and he's a candidate for God's grace. At that moment, God's healing can set in, God's forgiveness can take over, and the man can get what he asks for: pardon and healing and forgiveness.

Holy Father, keep them in the name.

VI

God's Destination For Man

"The God Movement is not something you enter into and flop down and say, 'God, I made it!' The God Movement isn't a sabbath in the sense of rest, or doing nothing; it is a sabbath in the sense of harmony, of tremendous activity— activity co-ordinated with God's purposes."

THE MEANING OF THE SABBATH

The Fourth Commandment says, "Remember the sabbath day to keep it holy." My father really drilled this into us. Keeping the sabbath day holy to him meant going to church in the morning and taking a good long nap in the afternoon. I remember all of us boys were out on the front lawn one Sunday afternoon while Dad was trying to get his nap and we were playing baseball. We were knocking it around and really whooping it up. Finally Dad came out there and said, "Don't you boys know this day is Sunday. If you're gonna play baseball, go out in back yard." Well, you see we were taught to observe the sabbath.

Now maybe we had better look at this thing a little more carefully. What does it mean? Remember the sabbath day to take a snooze? Is this what it is saying? "Remember the sabbath day to keep it holy; six days shalt thou labor." It looks like the six days of labor and the one day of rest are part of the same commandment. Isn't the command to labor just as much a part of the commandment as the commandment to rest?

This commandment was one of the most confusing ones to the Jews. I don't think they ever understood it. The only one who really understood it was Jesus and they didn't understand him. They jumped on him time and again on this very issue. But I think Jesus considered the "kingdom of God" or the "God Movement" to be a continuing way of life into which men would enter and I think he thought of this as the fulfillment of the sabbath. That was why he utterly disregarded the little concepts of the sabbath held by the religious people of his day.

One time he healed a fellow that was sick and told him to pick up his bed and go on home and these old church dignitaries just threw a tantrum. "He's taking his bed. He's working on the sabbath." They had worked so hard to define the sabbath and what work was. They had decided what the sabbath was. It was from sundown Friday to sundown Saturday. What they had trouble with was deciding what work was. They began to catalog all these things. For instance, they said that it was legal to feed your chickens bread on the sabbath but you couldn't feed them grain. The reason for this was that if you fed them grain somehow it might be missed by the old chicken and get under a leaf or a chip and it would sprout and come up and that would be planting on the sabbath. They also said that if a man with a wooden leg was in a house that caught fire on the sabbath it would be legal for him to come out of the house but he would have to take off his wooden leg, for if he came out with it, he would be carrying wood on the sabbath. They said that a woman could not look into a mirror on the sabbath. Now that was a tragic kind of ruling to put that kind of burden on a woman getting ready to go to church. But they would not let a woman look into a mirror on the sabbath. The reason, they said, was that she might spy a gray hair and pluck it out and that would be reaping.

These Hebrew people went to great length to define *work* and never did really succeed even though they had a tremendous catalog. Jesus just threw all that out the window and disregarded it. You remember that day he and his friends were walking through the grain field at just about dinner time on Sunday and nobody invited them home to dinner, so they plucked some grain and starting rubbing it out in their hands. Folks just raised cain about this because they thought that was combining on Sunday.

Jesus tried his best to answer these people but they never really accepted his understanding of what the sabbath was. He finally muzzled them I think, when he raised this question with them: "Is it lawful to do good or evil on the sabbath?" Now they translate the next as "and they were silent" but the Greek is a little more picturesque. It's, "and they were muzzled." Now what muzzled them? It was that little phrase, "on the sabbath." In other words if he had asked, "Is it lawful to do good or evil?" they could have answered him, "Why, to do good." But when he made morality or ethics dependent upon time, there was a confusing and impossible situation. If they had said, "It's lawful to do good on the sabbath," he would have said, "Well, get to work." If they had said, "It's lawful to do evil on the sabbath," he would have said, "How can a God of righteousness sanction evil at any time?" So they were muzzled.

I think we are muzzled when we fall into the same trap that the Pharisees fell into. Much of the Christian interpretation of the sabbath is simply going out into the junkyards of the Pharisees and bringing back stuff that Jesus swept out two millenniums ago. Well, what does it mean to keep the Sabbath? Here's what it says in Hebrews, chapter four:

Therefore it should really frighten us to realize that we, like them, are given an opportunity to enter his Promised Land with the same possibility that some of us might flub-the-dub. For we have had the news to fall on our ears the same as they. The reason it didn't do them one bit of good was because their hearing and their faith didn't connect. For it is only those who act on their convictions who enter the "sabbath," just like it says, "as I swore while provoked, they shall never enter into my sabbath although there had been an end of actual labor since the creation of the world."

Somewhere it says something like this about the seventh day, "And God entered on the seventh day into a state of rest from all his work," and then again it says, "They shall not enter my state of rest."

Since it is implied that some will enter and since those who were originally told about the Promised Land didn't make the grade because they lacked faith, God has decided to provide another opportunity which he calls today or now. Just as he said later in one of David's psalms, "Today if you are really serious about following him don't let your souls get calloused." For if Joshua had rested then, had sabbathed then, God wouldn't have spoken about still another day. You see then that a sabbath has been saved for God's people, for he who enters into his rest, God's rest, has ceased from his own activity as God did from his. Therefore let's put everything we've got into entering into that partnership so that none of us will fall into the same trap as those who, in the wilderness, would not trust him.

Now do you get that? *Sabbath* in the Greek means "to arrive at one's destination, to get where you're going." It means to quit worrying and struggling and striving and enter into a state of harmony and peace. It actually means a destination and it means entering into a partnership, a state of harmony with those who are there. Now when God created the heavens and the earth he didn't quit laboring. It says he entered into his destination.

What was the destination that he entered into? Sitting down and twiddling his thumbs and saying, "Well, I've got it all done now?" No. What did he do as the crowning act of his creation? He created what? *Man.* Now, the sabbath that God entered into was a union, a partnership with his chief creation, man. The sabbath that God had been aiming at was to cease from his own private, individual activities, for now he had a partner. Now he had a loved one and the "rest" that God entered into was the activity between him and his creation, Adam. This was God's sabbath. It was a partnership, a harmonious relationship that God entered into with his creature. Later Adam broke up the sabbath rest and God had to put him out of the sabbath.

The sabbath was in a sense the Old Testament equivalent of the Lord's Supper. It was to remind people that God's ultimate destination for man was harmony between him and his creation. The Promised Land was a symbol of the sabbath. And that's why it says that Joshua had "sabbathed" them. God swore they would never get into his sabbath, meaning that Promised Land where people would work together in harmony with their God. Later Joshua, who did want to go in, led the people into the Promised Land, but the tie had been broken.

The Hebrews saw this land of Canaan. What is our vision? The good news of the God Movement, the idea that God has a way of life for men which he is calling them to enter, in which they can reside in harmony with God's activity. The God Movement is not something you enter into and flop down and say, "God, I made it! From here on I've earned my right to my padded pew." The God Movement isn't a sabbath in the sense of rest, of doing nothing; it is a sabbath in the sense of harmony, of tremendous activity— activity co-ordinated with God's purposes.

This would really revolutionize our churches if they got that concept of the sabbath: that it is not a cessation of activity but the beginning of activity—activity synchronized to the will of God.

I overhauled an old tractor engine one time. When I got it back together the thing was out of time. I tried to crank it up and it went, "Bulp! Bulp! Bulp-bulp-bulp-bulp-bulp-bulp!" It just nearly flew to pieces, firing out of time. There was tremendous activity there, but it wasn't co-ordinated. Finally, when I got that thing perfectly timed, I cranked it up and it sounded good. "Purr-r-r-r-r." That old engine had entered its sabbath. It was in tune with the principles by which it was supposed to operate.

I imagine that is a pretty good symbol of the sabbath. It isn't inactivity, it's co-ordinated activity, activity co-ordinated to the purposes and will of God in history. So you enter the sabbath. You don't keep it; you live in it.

The object of the sabbath is that six days of labor. So then, when Jesus brings us into the sabbath, which is the kingdom of God, we cease from our own individual, private activity and become a part of a brotherhood. We cease from our own labors and give ourselves over to God to work with the brethren for the fulfillment of the kingdom of God on earth. We are truly praying for the sabbath when we say:

Thy kingdom come on earth as it is in heaven.

THE FATHER'S PURSUING LOVE

What about this view that the redemptive processes do go on beyond this earth? Does God still seek to redeem people even after they die; do we still have a chance to repent and respond to God's love? Now, of course, we're on very uncertain ground here. I'm not dogmatic at this point. But I do feel that it is important; it relates to an aspect of God that is important. How serious is he, really, about this business of redemption. How earnest, really, is his love? What kind of a God are we dealing with? This isn't just something for the theologians to debate. It really casts some light on the nature of God.

My response to this would be an effort to respond to the nature of God. Jesus' teaching was based on the nature of God. You love your enemies. Why? Because that's the way God acts. This is the way God has acted; so, therefore, this is the way you act. This is the sweep of the Fourth Commandment, to "remember the sabbath." And Jesus carried it out. We find him explaining certain attitudes, rooting them in God, and in the fifteenth chapter of Luke he tells three tremendous stories—all illuminating the nature of God. What set this off was that he was eating with publicans and sinners and people began to murmur and say, "Well, this isn't quite right on God's part. Here we are, we've been good religious people. We pray and we fast and we tithe, and here he is slighting us and going off with those publicans and those sinners and those harlots and all those folks. This guy isn't fair." So Jesus told three tremendous parables, all ending with the same theme.

One was the parable of the lost sheep. He said, "A certain shepherd had a hundred sheep and he lost one." Then he raises the question: "Will he not leave the 99 in the fold to go out and seek for the lost sheep. And when he has found it he lays it upon his shoulders and comes in and says 'Rejoice with me, I've found my sheep which was lost.' " He's saying God is like that shepherd. Now, how long did the shepherd search for the sheep? Until it got dark? No. Until he found it. How long is that? Just until he found it. Time is not in it, is it? It's the connection between the shepherd and the sheep that's the important thing. So, he's saying God's relationship to man is as timeless as the shepherd's relationship to his sheep.

Jesus told another story. He said, "It's like a woman who had ten coins and she lost one and. . . ." What does she do? She gets a broom. She sweeps and sweeps and sweeps. She lights up a lamp and sweeps until what? Until she wore her broom out? No. Until the lamp went out? No. Until her husband came home and said, "Hey, get my supper, what are you doing with that broom?" No. How long did she sweep? Until she found it. How long was that? As long as necessary.

"A certain man had two sons," Jesus said. "The younger said to his father, 'Father, give me that part of the inheritance that belongeth to me' and the father divided up his inheritance and after a while the younger boy took his leave into a foreign country." Now at that point, the father became dead. You could hurry on the death of your father by asking for a dividing up of the estate. You didn't have to wait until he died to divide it up. You could assume his death and ask him for a dividing up of the inheritance. But when you did that you assumed that you were dead to your father. So far as the relationship between you and your father was concerned from that point on, death had broken it. The father and the son were dead to one another. When the boy came home, the father said, "This my boy was dead and is alive." He was telling the truth. His son had been dead. The relationship had been a death relationship. Now, when the boy came to himself, he came home. How long did the father wait for him? Until he came home. Just that long. In the first two stories the father takes the initiative and in the last one the son has taken the initiative. The father's waiting is much more difficult than the active pursuit of the lost object. The waiting on the part of the father is infinitely more agonizing than is the activity of searching for sheep and sweeping for the coin.

What does this say to us about God? Doesn't it say to us that God in his relationship to us is not bound by time or circumstances? Suppose the shepherd had not found the sheep when the darkness of night descended, and the shepherd said, "Well, the darkness has overcome the light and I must go home. I have a lot of business." Are we dealing with that kind of a shepherd—one who lets darkness discourage him? Aren't we dealing with a shepherd who is not thwarted by the darkness of the night, nor the darkness of the grave? This is what the resurrection is trying to say to us—that the grave is not the final answer. The grave has been swallowed up in victory, death has lost its sting.

That the redemptive processes continue is quite evident in Rock's letter (I Peter). He claims that during this interval between the crucifixion and the resurrection Christ went and preached to the people in the other world. Why would he preach to them if there was no chance for their redemption?

Was Peter wrong? He seems to be saying that the redemptive

activity does continue beyond this physical life, that this earth is not the only stage for the drama of redemption, that the divine activity will continue in the life hereafter as he seeks to save those who are in Hades. (The word *Hades* in most instances simply means "the abode of the dead" and has nothing to do with punishment or reward.)

I think we got off the track with what may be a bad translation of this word *eon*. It's translated "eternal." It does have the aspect of timelessness in it, and in that respect could be translated as "eternal." But the idea of timelessness is not necessarily paramount in that word. The "eons" in the gnostic, Greek philosophy, were subdivine beings ruling over a certain period, or we would say, an "age." "Age"—or "eon"—refers to a quality or life rather than time. Take, for example, married life. How long is married life? Is it really a period of time? Can you say twenty years? Is it thirty years? Is it two years? Time isn't in it; "married life" refers to the quality or kind of life.

Now, this "eonian" life is the style and quality of life lived under God and with God. How long is it? We don't know. As long as necessary. In this case it would better be translated as "spiritual" life—he who believes in the Son has spiritual life. I think this would be a better translation than "eternal" or "everlasting." Luke eighteen reads: "Now a certain ruler asked him, saying, 'Good teacher, what shall I do that I might inherit *zōēn aiōnion?*'" That is translated there as "eternal life." It really means, "this quality of life that I see in you." This man was not interested in how he could get to heaven and live forever. He was asking, "How do I get the kind of life that I see in you and in those people about you?"

I just cannot stick my God into a little time-space relationship here, hindered and always working against the impending physical death. God is pursuing us. He pursues all men. It is not the will of God that any should perish. It's God's will to pursue us. He's pursuing us constantly. Some of us don't respond. We are loved with an unlimited love and with an everlasting love, but we're not sensitive to that love. Maybe God is in hot pursuit of us; we've been thinking about giving our heart to Christ. We're thinking so hard on it we're driving along and we don't hear the whistle of the freight train. And *bam* . . . it just smashes us to pieces. And God said, "You know, I almost had him. That freight train beat me to him." What kind of a God is that? A God whose purposes can be voided by a freight train? I can't fit that in.

I don't know what the afterlife is like. We have images and symbols that we can't rely on too much—talking about the golden streets and playing on the harps. Old John loves that kind of imagery and I can understand why. But I don't know that I want to spend eternity on a golden street. Gold's rather repulsive to me, anyway. I have never found much reason to seek for it and I don't want it. I don't want to walk on a golden street, and, for heaven's sake, I'd hate to think I'd have to spend eternity plunking on a harp. If that's going to be my destiny, I want to renegotiate this thing. But the thing that has meant the most to me in this life is to try to be an implement in God's hand, an agent of his in shedding his love abroad to people. That is my highest joy on earth. Would it not be my highest joy in the life hereafter? If God were to say to me, "Clarence, got a little job for you, fellow. You know that guy that was down there—he really was thinking very deeply, but that freight train got him?"

"Yeah, I do."

"He's off over there and he still isn't convinced that I love him. I wonder if you'd mind going over and seeing what you could do with him?"

"Ah, yes, sir. Thank you."

That prospect appeals to me. I don't know that I would enjoy the afterlife any more than to continue the redemptive activity that has been so blessed here on earth. Would it not be all the more blessed in the life hereafter? Are we going to get surly and say, "Well now, God, you gave him a chance. We had these churches here. He was at the revival meeting one time. He had a chance to believe, Lord, but he wouldn't believe. I think you ought to send him to hell. He had a chance."

Why? Why do we have to act with such surliness like the older brother did when the father says: "Bring the best robe, and put it on this boy"? This older brother says, "Man, look here. I've kept your will, I've obeyed you, I've been your slave all these years. You wouldn't even give me a little billygoat to have a party with my friends. But then when 'your son' comes home, you get a fatted calf for him. I don't get it. Nothing fair about this deal. It's unjust."

The old father said, "Look, everything I've got is yours. You're always with me. But when 'your brother' "—notice how the father throws it back—"when 'your brother' has come, I've just got to be happy. For he was lost and he's found. He was dead and is alive. Come on in. Come on in, son. Let's whoop it up. Cut out your surliness. Don't find fault with me about the fact that I want to love beyond anything that you know or can comprehend. Share in the joy of it."

Why should we find fault that God wants to extend the redemptive processes? Should that not be a cause of great rejoicing to us? If it's such a joy to win a soul on earth, why would it be any less of a joy to win it in the life hereafter? Would it really not be multiplied? Will we have a second chance? Of course. A third chance? Yes. A fifth chance. A thousandth chance. A millionth chance. A twin-quillion-billion-trillionth chance! For God will seek us—how long? Until he finds us. And when he's found the last little shriveling rebellious soul and has depopulated hell, then death will be swallowed up in victory, and Christ will turn over all things to the Father that he may be all and in all. Then every tongue shall confess that Jesus Christ is Lord, to the glory of God the Father.

I'm not objecting to as many chances as it takes to enfold a man into God's love that never quits. His love is such a precious thing to me that I covet it for all. God is not a celestial prison warden jangling the keys on a bunch of lifers—he's a shepherd seeking for sheep, a woman searching for coins, a father waiting for his son.

THE DEATH OF JESUS

I don't believe the crucifixion was the will of God. I've been asked: How do I fit that in with the Old Testament concept of shedding of blood for the sins of his people? Was not this God's son shedding his blood as a propitiation, so to speak, for the sins of the world?

Well, I believe that it was God's will that his son should be on this earth, that he should be in a crucifiable situation. I think the kind of life he lived was inevitably a life in the shadow of crucifixion. It was a life in such tension with the world—it was in mortal combat with the world—that either the world had to die or Jesus had to die. It was a fight unto death. And I think that God's way of love here is being a sin-bearer, of saying, "Sure, put on me your sin . . . let me be your scapegoat, let me be your lamb." Now this is the very important thing. For the cross is just this. It's saying to the world, "Now you have a cross, you have a sin-bearer. If you have sin, put it on."

The reason that the world is so terribly neurotic today is that it no longer has a sin-bearer. The Church doesn't want to bear the sins of the world. We don't want to be anybody's dumping ground. We don't want to have them throwing their dirty dishwater on us. And the world has no scapegoat; it has no sin-bearer. The body of Christ is unwilling to bear the sins of the world. But God was willing to bear. And so we throw on him our sins. Behold the Lamb of God, that taketh away in his own body, bearing our sins in his body up to the cross. Did God put our sins on the back of his son on the cross? No. He made him available and we put our sins on his back. Now, in the sense that God made Jesus available and expendable, God was a party to the crucifixion. Love makes itself available, love makes itself expendable.

I had this face me just a few weeks ago. The phone rang about 1:30 at night—we're used to all kinds of crank phone calls, usually they come late at night, and begin by somebody cussing you in a drunken tone. You generally let them talk—kind of discharge their static electricity or whatever it is that's motivating them. But this voice was very deliberate:

He said, "Who's speaking?"

I said, "Clarence Jordan."

He said, "Mr. Jordan, I just wanted to let you know that within about seventeen minutes there's going to be a green pickup truck pull out of that dirt road there just below the bridge and it's going to be loaded with dynamite. We haven't blown up your place with dynamite yet. Now we're going to blow it off the face of the map. I just wanted to call you to let you know so you would have time to get the people out of the buildings."

Well, I tell you, he scared the daylights out of me. I said, "Who's talking? Who am I speaking to?"

He said, "That isn't important."

I said, "But, brother, anyone who calls me at 1:30 at night to warn me to get these people out of the building, I owe him a debt of gratitude and I'd just like to know to whom am I grateful."

He said, *"I told you that isn't important and now you've got sixteen minutes."* BANG!

I'm standing there, 1:30 at night with a dead telephone in my hand, sixteen minutes to go. What are we going to do? The world's got to have somebody they can throw their sins on—even if it's dynamite. I stood there with that telephone in my hand, and about that time my boy called out to me and he said, "Who was it, Daddy?"

I said, "He wouldn't tell me."

"What did he want?"

"He wants to blow the place up."

He said, "Oh."

I went back to the bedroom and my wife said, "What's all that?"

I said, *"Some guy said he's going to blow this place up in sixteen minutes."*

She said, "Really?" and rolled over.

Here in an hour of crisis a man's closest don't seem to understand. They thought I was joking. "Oh?" "Really?" Well, I thought, if I were to go around to the other folks, banging on their doors and saying, "We're about to get blown up in sixteen minutes," they would say "Really?" I wouldn't get anywhere. So I crawled back into bed. I must confess the thoughts in my head were not conducive to sound slumber. I watched that clock click off those minutes. It clicked off sixteen minutes, and when it did headlights came up the road near that bridge and I thought, "Well, this is it." But we weren't going to be out there under that light, running around in our pajamas like a bunch of scared nitwits. We were going to be in our beds. And if the world wanted to have a little blowing-up party, they could have a little blowing-up party. It just could be, it'd do them good.

If this was the way God wanted to spend us, we had always said we were expendable, that it was his business as to how he wanted to expend us. If he wanted us to go up in one big flash, that was his business. In that respect the bombing would be the will of God. In that respect the crucifixion was the will of God. But it would not be God setting a match to the fuse. It is not God driving the nails. It isn't God driving the pickup truck. It's that God is making provision for the sins of the world to be discharged.

The pickup came up and slowed down, and I thought he was coming in. But he didn't. We felt this taunt that they threw at Jesus' face—"Let him save himself." He couldn't. He was the one that he couldn't save. He hadn't come in the first place to save himself. He'd come to save mankind. He was the only one who couldn't save himself. He could save others, but he could not save himself. The taunt was true. For the world had to have a lightning rod to discharge its static, spiritual energy. And God made himself available in his son. And I think God needs in this world, available people who will bear the sins of the world. Now that is what the death of Jesus means to me. He did die for our sins, and as a result of our sins. God made him available, but God didn't kill him. We did.

PERSISTING IN LOVE

In two great chapters of his first Letter to the Corinthians, chapters twelve and thirteen, Paul calls for a high level of Christian living and then gives the key for achieving it. In chapter twelve, verses one to three, we note that the people to whom Paul is speaking are people whose lives previously were dominated by false gods. He doesn't spell out who or what these gods were, but if these people at Corinth were anything like their contemporaries, the false gods had been Aphrodite, the goddess of love, or sex; Mammon, the god of money; Bacchus, the god of drink; and Caesar, the so-called divine head of the Roman government. But the Corinthians had had the good sense and the guts and the power from God to throw off these false gods.

More than that, they are people who have made an all-out commitment to God in Jesus Christ by making the great confession: "Jesus is Lord." When Paul was writing these words, the Roman government was demanding total loyalty and obedience from every citizen. In fact, the state had so exalted itself that it claimed that its head, the emperor, was divine and must be worshipped. The government set up images of the emperor throughout the empire and demanded that everyone give the loyalty oath by bending in front of the image and offering a pinch of incense to it, while saying, "Caesar *kurios*. . . . " Caesar is Lord. . . . The State is supreme." Now Christians could not commit such an act of blind patriotism, so they would simply stand before the image, offer no incense and say, "Jesus is Lord." Then they would be threatened, and unless they were willing to retract and say "Jesus be damned," they would be sentenced to death. So Paul is addressing people who not only have turned away from false gods, but who have committed themselves unto death to Jesus Christ.

But these people are not like peas in a pod, even though they are all sons of the same father. They're not spiritual twins. They don't all parrot the same jargon. True, they share a common spirit, but this doesn't mean that they are all exactly alike. They have different abilities, different outlooks, different backgrounds, different racial ancestry, and, possibly, different hair cuts. And because of these differences one might conclude that they are not all following the same God. But Paul thinks otherwise. He readily admits the differences, but underneath he sees a high degree of unity.

In verses four to six he compares the Christian fellowship to a body which has many different parts, each of which performs its own specialized function, doing so, however, within the frame-work of the larger whole, and for the benefit of the entire body. In fact, Paul feels that these differences are absolutely essential to the health and usefulness of not only the whole body, but also of the individual part itself. This is the way he puts it in chapter twelve, verses twelve to twenty-one:

It's just like the body which is entire within itself, even though it has many parts. With all its parts, it is still only one body. That's the way it is with Christ. For through one spirit we all, whether white or Negroes, laborers or white-collar workers, we all were initiated into one body and all of us had one spirit breathed into us. For the body does not consist of just one part, but many. If the foot should say, "Since I'm not a hand, I don't belong to the body," would this make it so? Or if the ears should say, "Since I'm not an eye, I don't belong to the body," would this make it so? If the whole body were an eye, how could it hear? Or if it were an ear, how could it smell? But as it is, God has arranged every single part of the body according to his own design. If every-thing consisted of just one part, how could it be a body? Now, indeed, the parts are many, but the body is a unit. So, then, the eye can't say to the hand, "I don't need you." Nor again can the head say to the foot, "I don't need you."

From this it is clear that Christ's body has many parts, and that each part needs the other. One part might consist of white peo-ple, another Negroes. One part may consist of laborers, another white-collar workers. One part may be educated. Another part illiterate. One part might live in the slums, and another in the suburbs. But all are parts of the same body and none can exist independently of the other. When one group says to another, "We don't want you," it is maiming the entire body of Christ . . . de-stroying its usefulness, and ultimately bringing about its own destruction. To open our doors and joyfully receive its brothers—all the other parts of Christ's body—is not only wise, but utterly essential to our own health.

In the light of this, then, we may safely say that any church which ushers a man out because of the color of his skin, or any person who turns away from his brother because of a different economic or educational background, or anyone who by the tone of his voice pours contempt upon his brother, is thereby alienat-ing himself from the body of Christ . . . and bringing about his own destruction.

So, here is this strange hodgepodge of parts—this classless, caste-less, raceless fellowship called the Body of Christ. What holds it together? What brings order out of its chaos? What prevents it from being torn asunder from inner conflict? What gives it symmetry, co-ordination, and power? It's just one word: love. Love is the lifeblood of the body, coursing through every part, bringing to it health and life. Without it, the entire body soon decomposes into a stinking mass. It becomes worse than nothing.

In First Corinthians, chapter thirteen, verses one through three, Paul strikingly sets forth the meaninglessness and the futility of life without love. He says:

Though I speak with the tongues of men and of angels but have no love, I am a hollow sounding horn, or a nerve-wracking rattle. And though I have the ability to preach and know all the secrets and all the slogans and though I have sufficient faith to move a mountain, but have no love, I am nothing. And though I renounce all my possessions and though I give my body as a flaming sacrifice but have not love, I accomplish exactly nothing.

It's not enough, then, for a fellowship merely to integrate or just tolerate one another. We must open our hearts to God's love and let it flow into us and then through us to all of our brothers about us. With this love alive, when this love is alive in our hearts, how does it express itself? Paul tells us, in chapter thirteen, verses four to seven,

Love is long-suffering and kind. Love is not envious, nor does it strut and brag.

Perhaps brag about how superior it is, or how it's strong enough enough to blow somebody off the face of the map.

It does not act up nor try to get things for itself. It pitches no tantrums.

And today Paul might say, "And it drops no bombs on cities and it drops no napalm on villages."

It pitches no tantrums . . . it keeps no books on insults or injuries. Sees no fun in wickedness, but rejoices when truth (not progaganda) *prevails. Love is all embracing, all trusting, all hoping, all enduring. Love never quits.*

This, then, is the way love behaves and if we're to be people of love, we must order our lives along these lines. Even though people about us choose the path of hate and violence and warfare and greed and prejudice, we who are Christ's body must throw off these poisons and let love permeate and cleanse every tissue and cell. Nor are we to allow ourselves to become easily discouraged when love is not always obviously successful or pleasant. Love never quits, even when an enemy has hit you on the right cheek and you have turned the other, and he's also hit that. Love continues to forgive not only when a brother has sinned against you seven times, but seventy times seven. Love doesn't quit or give up on a man whether he be a Communist or a Kluxer. Christ showed us how far love would go when he prayed for those who were driving the nails into his hands and said, "Father forgive them, for they don't know what they're up to."

Now it is obvious that this life of love is not for children. It is entirely too difficult for weaklings and cowards. It is not given to those who chicken out. It is for those strong, brave, souls who wish to grow into the fullness of the stature of Jesus Christ. Love is the mark of spiritual maturity, the evidence that we have passed from childhood to manhood. Paul puts it this way in chapter thirteen, verses eleven and twelve. He said:

For example, when I was a child I was talking like a child, thinking like a child, acting like a child, but when I became an adult I outgrew my childish ways. For until now (that is, without love) *it's like looking at one another in a trick mirror. But then,* (that is, with love) *we see eye to eye. Up until this point* (that is, without love) *I understand immaturely. But then* (that is, with love) *I shall understand in the same way that I shall be understood.*

Now, it's perfectly natural for a child to act in childish ways, but something's wrong when an adult acts in childish ways. The Christian must be no stunted runt but a full-grown son of God. This is what Jesus is saying in Matthew, chapter five, verses forty-six to forty-eight:

For if you love those who love you, what's your advantage? Don't even scalawags do that? You-all, therefore, must be mature, just as your spiritual father is mature.

Jesus isn't ordering us to be perfect, but he is letting us know that the Father expects us to grow up. Paul says that without love we are like people who are looking at each other in a trick mirror. I was once at the Ripley Museum in Niagara Falls, Canada, and there I visited the Hall of Mirrors. There were all kinds of trick mirrors which could distort the body into almost any conceivable form. When looking into one of them you would appear tall and skinny. Other mirrors could make a person appear flatheaded, big-eared, round as a ball, or hopelessly deformed. I think that Paul is suggesting that if we look at people through anything other than the clear glass of love, they may appear to be brutes, hostile strangers, worthless animals or loathsome scum. But if we view them through Christ's love, it is like seeing eye to eye with no distortion. Then we can understand others even as God in Jesus Christ understood us.

People today are being bombarded with all kinds of high pressure commercials urging them to get a certain kind of cigarette because it's cooler or smoother or longer. Or, if they were truthful, more deadly than others. We're told to get a certain kind of automobile because it's slicker or faster or wider. We must hurry and get the only mouthwash that will keep our breath sweet all day. Paul would remind us that few things really have enduring value. In fact, he mentions only three. He says:

Now these three things endure: Faith, Hope, and Love. But the greatest of all is Love. Seek diligently for Love.

A SPIRIT OF PARTNERSHIP

When the time is ripe, says God, I will shed my spirit on all mankind.
And your sons and your daughters will speak truthfully.
Your young people will come up with starry ideas,
And your old people will have radical suggestions.
Yes indeed, when the time is ripe I'll shed my spirit
On my boys and my girls and they will speak the truth.
And I will put terror in the sky above
And nightmares on the earth below—
Blood and fire and a mushroom cloud.
The sun will be turned into blackness
And the moon into blood.
And then our eyes shall see the glory
Of the coming of the Lord.
At that time, everyone who relies on the nature of the Lord will be rescued.

"I will shed my spirit on all mankind." A spirit of partnership. The rich man will sit down at the same table with a poor man and learn how good cornbread and collard greens are, and the poor man will find out what a T-bone steak tastes like. Neither will shiver in a drafty house, nor have to move his furniture when it rains. Both will rejoice in the robust health of their children, who are not listless from having too little nor bored from having too much. They will discover the blessedness of sharing, the warmth of compassion, the quiet strength of humility, and the glow of gentleness, the cleanness of honesty, the peace of justice, the ecstasy of love. God's spirit will let a white man look into the eyes of a black man and see his soul; it will let a black man look into the eyes of a white man and see his soul. And they'll both know it's the soul of a man.

God's spirit will teach an educated man and an uneducated man to walk together in the cool of the evening after a hard day's work and both will know that one could not live without the other. One will not ask for more than his share and the other need not accept less than his share. Each will delight in the skills of his brother, and neither will exploit the other's weakness.

God's spirit will call the people from the East to join hands with the people from the West, and the people from the North to join hands with the people from the South and all will seek the other's good. None will smite his brother, nor deal deceitfully. They will sing at their labors, and be thankful for the fruits of the fields and factories. Their soldiers will learn the arts of peace; their strong men the ways of service. All will be spared the degradation of making implements of war and the agonizing shame of using them.

God's spirit will join an old man's wisdom with a young man's strength and they will be partners for the Lord. They will respect one another, and will be slow to take offense and quick to forgive. They will be as father and son. The old man will be filled with compassion and understanding, and the young man with gentleness and loving concern. They will find joy in bearing one another's burdens.

God's spirit will give eyes to mankind with which to see the glory of the Lord. God's spirit will give ears to mankind to hear the sound of his trumpet as well as his still small voice. He will dwell with us and be our God, and we shall be his people. He will wipe away our tears, dispel our doubt, remove our fears, and lead us out. He will heal the brokenhearted, open the eyes of the blind, release the captives, preach the good news to the poor, and usher in the acceptable year of the Lord. He will bulldoze the mountains and fill in the valleys, he will make the rough places smooth and the crooked ways straight. He'll stand every man on his feet so that all mankind may see his glory together.